Jam, Jelly & Relish

Jam, Jelly & Relish

SIMPLE PRESERVES, PICKLES & CHUTNEYS
& CREATIVE WAYS TO COOK WITH THEM

Ghillie James

PHOTOGRAPHS BY LAURA HYND
KYLE BOOKS

Dedicated to three inspiring women—my two grandmothers Margaret and Isobel (Sybil) and my mother Jane. Written for Andrew, William, and our newly born Jemima.

Kyle Books
an imprint of Kyle Cathie Limited
www.kylebooks.com
Distributed by National Book Network
4501 Forbes Blvd. Suite 200
Lanham, MD 20706
(800) 462-6420

First published in Great Britain in 2010 by Kyle Cathie Limited

ISBN 978-1-906868-18-5

10 9 8 7 6 5 4 3 2 1

Text © 2010 Ghillie James
Design © 2010 Kyle Cathie Limited
Photographs © 2010 Laura Hynd

The recipes in this book have been developed and tested in a home kitchen. Although every effort has been made to convey these recipes as risk-free as possible, the author and publisher assume no responsibility for damages associated with the use of this book.

PROJECT EDITOR Jenny Wheatley
PHOTOGRAPHER Laura Hynd
DESIGNER Jim Smith
HOME ECONOMISTS Ghillie James, Annie Rigg, Sonja Edridge and Karen Pilkington
STYLIST Cynthia Inions
COPY EDITOR Anne McDowall
EDITORIAL ASSISTANT Catharine Robertson
PRODUCTION Gemma John

Library of Congress Control Number: 2011920343

Color reproduction by Scanhouse
Printed and bound in China by C&C Offset Printing Company Ltd.

Contents

INTRODUCTION:
THE STICKY BUSINESS OF PRESERVING

Sitting at a kitchen table and finding a jar with a hand-written label always fills me with a sure feeling that there is a good cook in the house. A bottle of homemade ketchup to smother over sausages for lunch, or some blackberry jelly for toasted muffins—this, to me, is what comfort food is all about. And yet so many of us seasoned cooks (myself included) haven't tried preserving...at least not until now!

My aim in writing this book was to try to dispel the myth that preserving is a task requiring a degree. To me, it was in the same class as sugar spinning and chocolate tempering—cooking's version of algebra, something a few people "get" but others are left to struggle with. I also had the idea that I would need to stock up on a mass of expensive specialist equipment that would be used once before being left to gather dust at the back of a cupboard. How wrong I was: in fact, preserving couldn't be simpler.

I hope that I have been able to establish, through trial and error, what equipment is essential and what you can dispense with, and that the recipes will reassure you that home preserving is neither time consuming or complicated. I've avoided the overly complex jargon that often seems to blight preserve recipes, and have also reduced timings where possible. Here, then, are some simple instructions for failsafe preserving, with some really tasty flavor combinations and ideas for up-to-date and useful preserves.

I come from a family that's totally obsessed with food—as a two-year-old I used to make meringues in the bath using a whisk, a bowl, and a lot of bath foam! Now I have my own family, and we love to eat what's at its tastiest each month. But so often the most flavorsome foods are quick to vanish—the sweetest, juiciest blackberries in the bushes are soon nibbled by the birds, while a glut of the ripest home-grown tomatoes gives way to dull, tasteless supermarket ones

in what seems like days. One thing I adore about preserving is that you can capture each season at its best, keeping in tune with the rhythm of nature. Without cheating the seasons, you can recreate the richness of summer just by opening a jar. There is nothing better to brighten a Sunday lunch than a warm upside-down cake bursting with the flavor of Seville orange marmalade .

Whether you are lucky enough to have a vegetable garden brimming with zucchini plants or just a great local farmers' market stocked with fruits and veggies at their peak, you can store the best the seasons have to offer, when produce is at its cheapest and most abundant. In doing so, you will also be cutting down on food miles—something we are all conscious of in our environmentally focused age.

I also wanted to ensure that this book provides more than simply preserving recipes, and so I have also included recipes that offer creative ways to cook with your bottles and jars of seasonal goodies. There is, after all, only so much poached rhubarb a girl should eat, but when it can be quickly turned into a delicious dinner party dessert for friends, you suddenly have a really useful shelf of tricks.

I hope that you enjoy it.

Ghillie

EQUIPMENT AND USEFUL INFORMATION

Here is a (hopefully) surprisingly short list of simple rules and essential equipment for successful preserving.

Pots, pans, and jars

There are a huge number of gadgets and machines available that aim to make jam making easy for you—my father swears by his jam maker, for example. However, if you are a beginner and/or attempting to economize by using the season's harvest, it seems rather pointless spending money on unnecessary equipment. I have two very large saucepans (not specifically preserving ones, but deep enough to hold a good quantity and have some space at the top for boiling) that I use for everything, plus a cheap and cheerful jelly strainer and jam funnel bought online (see list of suppliers on page 170).

I tend to use a few ½ quart (500ml) mason jars (great tied with a pretty luggage tag and a piece of patterned ribbon for presents), as well as an odds-and-ends assortment of jars that I keep in my cupboard. Ensure that the lids seal onto the jars tightly—older jars tend to lose their grip and eventually start to rust and these will just contaminate the preserves. Mason jars with rubber seals or a two-part top are best for any preserves that require heat treatment in the oven as these can withstand the temperatures required.

The capacity of some jars is given by volume (mason jars, for example, come as ml or quarts/liters), others by weight (i.e. g, oz, or lb). In the recipes, I've given approximate yields in quarts, but when making jam, you'll find that this does vary. You may want to pour your jam into a big measuring pitcher first so that you know exactly how much you have made. You can then collect up the jars in your cupboard and ensure you have the right number.

The other gadget I have found to be a huge help (though not essential) when it comes to slicing peel for marmalade and chopping ingredients for chutneys is my food processor. I have one with a blade and a slicer attachment, but most will do the job perfectly well.

Sterilizing jars

It is essential to sterilize your jars or bottles before you fill and seal them in order to destroy any micro-organisms that might otherwise contaminate your preserves. I find the oven method below the easiest way to do this because you can simply put the jars on a baking sheet in the oven as your preserve is resting, rather than having to either boil and dry them all or wait for the dishwasher to end its cycle. However, you can bring the jars up to a boil in a pan of water or put them through a very hot dishwasher cycle if you prefer. You will need to make sure they have air dried just before filling though, as they should be warm when filled.

To sterilize jars and bottles in the oven, preheat it to 300°F (150°C). Wash the jars in hot soapy water until spotlessly clean, then dry them with a clean kitchen towel, place them onto a baking sheet, and put in the oven for 5 minutes. Remove the jars from the oven and fill and seal while both the preserve and the jars are still warm.

Some jars and bottles have lids with plastic seals, which will melt if put into the oven. You can sterilize them by washing them in hot soapy water then transferring them to a bucket of sterilizing solution for the allocated time.

Mason jars that are being used for poaching fruits don't require drying before filling. I find the easiest way to sterilize them is to bring them and their rubber seals up to a boil in a large pan of water and then simply remove them with tongs when you're ready to fill them.

Using a jelly bag

Various members of my family use anything from an old pillowcase to some clean tights to strain their jelly! Call me extravagant, but I do think that spending a small amount on buying a jelly bag on a stand (pictured right) is worth the expense! There's not a lot to using one, but remember that if you squeeze it to eke out more juice, your jelly might end up a bit cloudy.

When boiling jelly, you might find it produces a bit of residue. If there's only a small amount, you can remove it by simply wiping a piece of paper towel over the surface. Skim off larger amounts using the edge of a spoon.

Achieving a good set

Setting point is achieved once a jam or jelly has been cooking for long enough to reach 220°F (105°C). In order to achieve this, once the sugar has dissolved, you need to increase the heat to its highest setting and allow the mixture to come up to a "rolling boil." At this point the jam or jelly will be covered with a mass of vigorously boiling bubbles and it will look as though there's a real swell on the surface. The aim is to keep the temperature of the mixture as consistently high as possible—but without it boiling over and making a mess of your stove!

If you have a jam thermometer, by all means, use it. Personally, I find standing over a steamy pot attempting to look at a cloudy hot tube a waste of time but, if you prefer, then do use a thermometer to test whether your jam has reached setting point rather than using the method given on the right.

Once the jam or jelly has been boiling for long enough, the mixture will begin to look more glossy and less watery than before; it is at this point that you need to start testing for a set (see box). I have given a suggested timing in each recipe but, as mentioned opposite, this can vary, depending on your pan, your burner, and the ripeness and variety of fruit used. If you think your jam might be ready, don't wait—test it! Equally, don't panic if your jam is taking longer to set. Just go with your instinct, keep checking it every few minutes and don't rush it—it will reach setting point eventually! Achieving a good set requires patience but, once you start testing, it's important to work quickly.

Jams and jellies will firm up quite a lot more in their jars as they cool, and you will often find that they will set further after a day or so of being left in a cool place.

To test for a set:

- Put 3 or 4 small plates or saucers in the fridge as you begin your recipe.
- Keep the jam gently boiling.
- When you are ready to test for a set, remove a chilled plate from the fridge and spoon a small amount of jam (a tablespoonful or so) onto it.
- Return the plate to the fridge for about 30 seconds.
- Remove the plate and run your finger through the middle of the jam.
- If the jam or jelly is ready it should clearly wrinkle, as if beginning to set.
- If it is still smooth, turn the heat back up and leave to cook for 3 minutes longer and test again, using a new chilled plate.

Variations in setting times

Timings for setting seem to vary no matter how much a recipe is tested and it seems that there's no hard and fast rule to help—just don't panic! Slightly underripe fruit sets better as it contains a higher level of pectin (the natural setting agent found in fruit), but varieties of fruit seem to make a big difference, too—my strawberry jam took anything from 8 to 25 minutes in testing!

Through trial and error, I've found that the easiest and tastiest method of making jams from a fruit with a low-to-medium pectin content is to either pair it with a fruit with a high pectin content or to add liquid or powdered pectin to the juice before boiling. Pectin can be found in most supermarkets; be sure to follow package instructions in order to help your jam achieve a set.

The recipes in this book generally have a lower sugar content and thus a more fruity flavor. Personally, I think that a jam is ruined when it's too firm and sweet.

How to tell if a relish or chutney is ready

As you approach the end of the cooking time, you will find that the relish or chutney gets thicker at the bottom of the pan, and you will need to stir it more regularly to keep it from sticking. It often resembles a trembling volcano, so watch you don't get spat at!

The easiest way to tell if it's cooked is to run a wooden spoon through the middle of the pan. The spoon should leave a trail behind it and, yet, this should fill quickly with liquid. Remember that the chutney will thicken as it cools: you don't want it to be too dry.

Filling jars

Don't attempt to use a spoon to fill your jars or you will be there for days. I find a jam funnel incredibly handy—then you can simply ladle in the preserve or pour from a pitcher.

Storing preserves

Unless otherwise stated, store your sealed jars and bottles in a cool dark, dry place. A garage is great, otherwise just anywhere that doesn't get too hot or damp. Once opened, all jars and bottles should be kept in the fridge.

Seasonal Chart

These lists of what's in season when will indicate whether your fruit and vegetables are a local or imported crop and will hopefully help you plan your preserve making throughout the year. Bear in mind, however, that harvesting times do vary from year to year.

Early spring
Clementines
Lemons
Rhubarb
Passion fruit

Late spring
Apricots
Asparagus
Elderflowers
Rhubarb
Strawberries
Watercress
Mint
Pineapple
Sage
Tarragon
Thyme
Rosemary

Early summer
Apricots
Asparagus
Basil
Beets
Blackberries
Blackcurrants
Blueberries
Carrots
Cherries
Chili peppers
Cucumbers
Elderflowers
Gooseberries
Lavender
Mangoes
Mint
Nectarines
Pineapple

Plums
Radishes
Redcurrants
Rosemary
Rhubarb
Sage
Strawberries
Tarragon
Thyme
Zucchini

Late summer
Basil
Beets
Blackberries
Blackcurrants
Blueberries
Carrots
Cherries
Chili peppers
Cucumbers
Green beans
Lavender
Mangoes
Nectarines
Onions
Peaches
Peppers
Plums
Radishes

Raspberries
Redcurrants
Rosemary
Sage
Shallots
Strawberries
Sweet corn
Tomatoes
Thyme
Zucchini

Early autumn
Apples (eating
   and cooking)
Beets
Blueberries
Carrots
Green beans
Onions
Peaches
Pears
Peppers
Radishes

Raspberries
Shallots
Tomatoes/green
   tomatoes
Zucchini

Late autumn
Apples (eating
   and cooking)
Carrots
Fennel
Lemons
Nuts
Pears
Raspberries
Red cabbage

Early winter
Apples (eating
   and cooking)
Carrots
Lemons
Cranberries
Clementines
Grapefruit
Nuts
Pineapple
Red cabbage

Late winter
Clementines
Cranberries
Grapefruit
Lemons
Limes
Oranges (Seville
   and Blood)
Pineapple
Passion fruit
Red cabbage

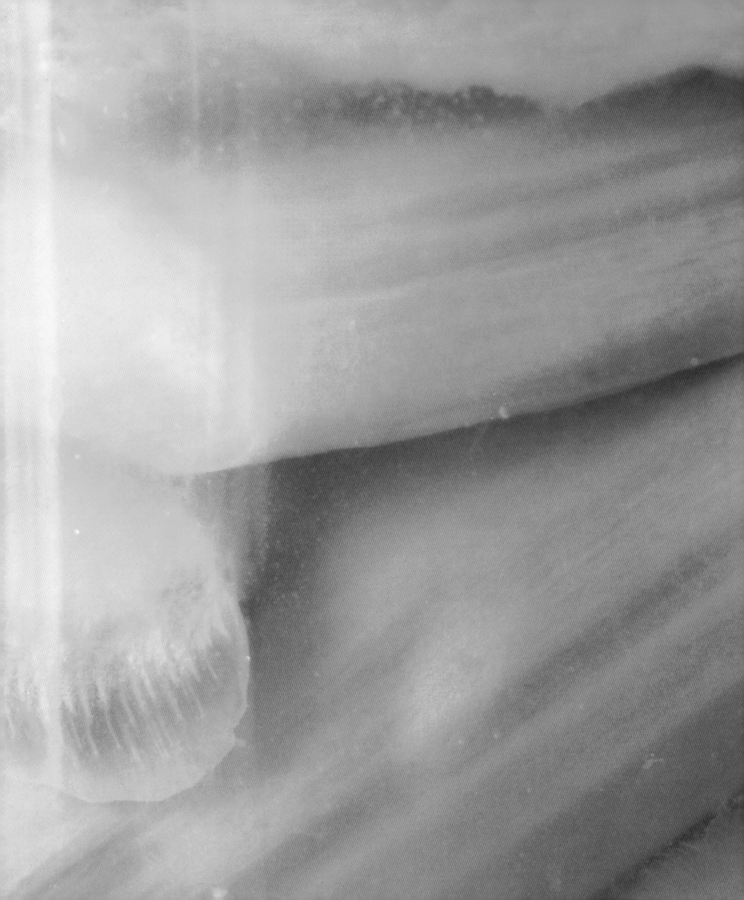

Spring

Rhubarb and Early Strawberry Jam

The combination of rhubarb and strawberries is delicious. Although early strawberries are a little less flavorful than later varieties, they are fine when used in a mix, but you can, of course, use later strawberries for this recipe too, with frozen rhubarb chunks if you can't get fresh. Strawberry jam can be a little troublesome when it comes to setting; the timings for reaching setting point given here are therefore just a guide, and you might find your jam needs more or less boiling time.

Makes about 2½ quarts (1.8 liters)
Keeps for at least a year

1½lb (800g) rhubarb, trimmed and cut into 1in (2.5cm) chunks
1lb (500g) strawberries, not too ripe, sliced
   or halved, depending on size
juice of 2 large lemons
6 cups granulated sugar
liquid or powdered pectin (optional): use according to
   package instructions if set is not achieved

Put all the ingredients into a bowl and stir. Leave the mixture to macerate for 2 hours, which will give the fruit time to release its juices.

Transfer the mixture to a large pan and slowly dissolve the sugar, stirring over medium heat. Leave the fruit to simmer for another 10 minutes, then increase the heat to a rolling boil and cook for about 15 minutes, or until you think setting point has been reached. If it needs longer, just keep it boiling and test again.

Remove the pan from the heat and leave to rest for 15 minutes. Skim off any residue with the edge of a spoon, then pour the jam into warm sterilized jars and seal them.

Poached Rhubarb with Orange and Ginger Wine

Rhubarb freezes beautifully, so you might prefer to poach it as needed straight from the freezer. However, freezer space can be limited, and time, precious. This recipe enables you to make a big batch in one go and forget about cooking when you don't feel up to it. Rhubarb, orange, and ginger make a wonderful combination: the spice and orange add warmth to the refreshing rhubarb. You can use water instead of the ginger wine. Don't be surprised if the rhubarb loses a bit of color during baking.

Makes about 1½ quarts (1.5 liters)
Keeps for up to 6 months
1½ to 1¾ cups superfine sugar
juice of 3 smallish oranges
½ cup ginger wine
2lb (1kg) rhubarb, trimmed and cut into 2in (5cm) chunks

Use large mason jars for this recipe, for ease of packing in the chunks of rhubarb and because they can withstand the temperature required for heat treatment. Preheat the oven to 300°F (150°C).

Put the sugar and 2 cups water into a pan and heat gently until the sugar has dissolved. If you are using the bright pink forced rhubarb, which is a little less tart, use only 1½ cups sugar. Increase the heat and boil for 1 minute.

Put the jars in the oven and heat for 5 minutes. Add the orange juice to the syrup and simmer for 10 minutes, then add the wine and turn off the heat. Pack the rhubarb tightly into the jars, then pour in the hot syrup until it reaches the top. Rest the lids on top of the jars without sealing.

Lay a dish cloth or kitchen towel on the bottom of a roasting pan. Put the filled jars on top, spacing them well apart, and add 1in (2.5cm) boiling water to the pan. Put into the oven for 25 to 30 minutes or until the rhubarb is tender, but still retains its shape. Remove the jars from the oven and seal immediately.

LEMON AND PASSION FRUIT POTS WITH RHUBARB

This is a really easy dessert to prepare; you can make it ahead of time and simply finish it off with the gingersnap crumbs just before serving. The creamy lemon is really just a classic lemon posset with some passion fruit mixed in. The poached rhubarb at the bottom adds a refreshing surprise and makes these fruit pots slightly less rich.

Serves 6
2 cups heavy cream
½ cup superfine sugar
juice of 2 lemons
pulp of 2 passion fruit
13oz (375g) Poached Rhubarb with Orange and Ginger Wine (see left) or 6 heaping tablespoons freshly poached and sweetened rhubarb
3 gingersnap cookies

Add the cream and sugar to a pan and bring to a boil, then keep at a boil for 3 minutes.

In a bowl, stir together the lemon juice and passion fruit pulp. Whisk into the cream (while it is still hot) and leave to stand for 15 minutes. Meanwhile, spoon the poached rhubarb into the bottoms of 6 x ½ cup ramekins.

Slowly pour the cream on top of the rhubarb in each ramekin. Cool and chill for 2 to 3 hours.

To prepare the topping, put the gingersnaps into a food processor and pulse until crushed. (Alternatively, put them into a plastic bag and crush with a rolling pin.) Top the creams with the crushed gingersnap cookies just before serving.

Elderflower Cordial

I now always think of my goddaughter Alice when I make elderflower cordial because I was making it on the day she was born. It is quite addictive served with sparkling water and is also a heavenly addition to many summer cocktails, such as Elderflower and Rum Fizz (see right). Unfortunately, I have found the odd moldy bottle in the past, so store bottles in the fridge or freezer.

Makes about 2½ quarts (2.5 liters)
Keeps indefinitely in the freezer
or up to 6 months in the fridge

9 cups granulated sugar
zest and juice of 2 lemons
50 elderflower heads, shaken to remove any creatures
2oz (50g) citric acid

Put the sugar into a large non-metallic container and pour in 1½ quarts (1.5 liters) boiling water. Stir to dissolve, then add the lemon zest and juice, elderflower heads, and citric acid. Leave overnight.

Strain through a jelly strainer or a cheesecloth-lined sieve. Pour the cordial into warm sterilized bottles (three-quarters full if you are freezing them) and seal.

ELDERFLOWER AND RUM FIZZ

This is a cross between a Mojito and a Pimm's—really refreshing and very addictive. Increase the quantities and make it in large pitchers for a party: put a fresh mint sprig in each glass prior to guests arriving, then just add ice and pour in the fizz.

Makes 2 glasses

12 mint leaves
¼ cup Elderflower Cordial (see left)
⅓ cup rum
2 tablespoons lemon juice
1 cup sparkling water
ice and 2 mint sprigs, to serve

Put the mint leaves and elderflower cordial into a glass pitcher and mash with the end of a rolling pin to release the oils from the herbs. Add the rum and lemon juice and stir.

Top off with sparkling water then pour into 2 glasses that are half full of ice, holding the mint aside with the back of a spoon. Garnish with a mint sprig and serve.

APPLE AND ELDERFLOWER PIE

This recipe could just as easily sit in the autumn chapter, as Macintosh apples are falling off the trees at the end of autumn and you might have a stash of elderflower cordial left from the spring harvest. I saw cream cheese added to sweet pastry in a recipe a while ago, but this is the first time I have tried it myself—it adds a lightness and works beautifully with the apples.

Serves 6 to 8

For the pastry

2½ cups all-purpose flour

2 tablespoons superfine sugar, plus a little extra for dusting

8 tablespoons (1 stick) butter, chilled, cut into cubes

¼ cup cream cheese

For the filling

4lb (1.8kg) cooking apples, peeled, cored, and cut into thin slices

¾ cup superfine sugar

2 heaping tablespoons all-purpose flour

4 tablespoons Elderflower Cordial (see page 25)

1 egg, beaten, to glaze

To make the pastry, put all the ingredients into a food processor and blend, adding a little water to bring the mixture together. Turn the dough onto a floured surface and form into a circle, then wrap in plastic wrap and chill for at least 2 hours, or overnight.

When you are ready to make the pie, combine the apples, sugar, flour, and elderflower cordial in a bowl, tossing together to mix thoroughly. Turn into a deep pie dish (about 9in/23cm diameter and 2in/5cm deep) so that the apples pile up.

On a floured surface, gently roll out the pastry until about ¼in (5–7mm) thick, being careful not to stretch the pastry as you roll. Cut ¾in (2cm) strips from around the outside of the pastry, brush the rim of the dish with a little water, and stick the pastry strips to it, pressing down. Brush a little water over this pastry edge, then place the whole piece of remaining pastry over the filled dish, pressing down around the edge to seal. Brush the top of the pie with the beaten egg, sprinkle with sugar, and cut 4 steam holes in the top. Chill for up to 2 hours or until ready to cook.

Preheat the oven to 350°F (180°C). Bake the pie for 35 to 40 minutes or until deep golden. Serve with vanilla ice cream.

Curried Rhubarb Chutney

This chutney is the result of a visit to friends, who asked me if I could recreate a delicious mildly curried rhubarb relish that they had recently tasted. It's a great savory use for rhubarb.

Makes about 1¼ quarts (1.25 liters)
Keeps for at least a year

2lb (1kg) rhubarb, cut into 2in (5cm) pieces

1 large onion, peeled and finely chopped

6 or 7 pitted dates, chopped

¾ cup golden raisins

1½ cups light brown sugar

¼ cup honey

2 to 3 teaspoons (depending on how hot
   you like it) hot curry paste (I used Madras)

1 teaspoon sea salt

½ teaspoon ground coriander

½ teaspoon ground cumin

½ teaspoon mixed spice (try a blend of ground coriander,
   cinnamon, cloves, ginger, and nutmeg)

1⅔ cups cider vinegar

Put all the ingredients into a large pan with 1 cup water. Cook over medium heat, stirring occasionally, until the mixture thickens and leaves a trail when stirred with a wooden spoon (this will take 1½ to 2 hours). As the mixture cooks, the liquid will rise to the surface, with the chutney thickening at the bottom of the pan, so continue to stir every so often until the liquid has reduced to the point that it feels and looks less like a sauce and has formed the consistency of a chutney. Pour it into warm sterilized jars and seal. Leave to mature for 4 weeks before eating.

Mango Chutney

We get through buckets of mango chutney in our house but the brands that we really love are very expensive. My solution is to make a good-sized batch, which we can then eat to our hearts' content! Feel free to halve this quantity if you wish—simply adjust the end cooking time accordingly.

Makes about 4 quarts (4 liters)

Keeps for at least a year

For the toasting spices

15 cardamom pods

¾ teaspoon ground cloves

½ heaping teaspoon nigella
   or kalonji (black onion) seeds

½ heaping teaspoon fenugreek

½ teaspoon crushed red pepper flakes

2 red onions, peeled and chopped

4 garlic cloves, peeled and sliced

1 cinnamon stick

2½ cups cider vinegar

8 large underripe mangoes

3 large cooking apples, peeled,
   cored and sliced

4½ cups packed light brown sugar

Put all the toasting spices into a small frying pan and toast over low heat, stirring, until they release their spicy aromas.

Add the toasted spices to a large pan with the onions, garlic, cinnamon stick, and vinegar and simmer for 10 minutes.

While the onions soften, peel the mangoes using a potato peeler and, using a sharp knife, remove the flesh on either side of the pits. Cut the flesh into ½in (1cm)-thick lengths, then halve each lengthwise. Remove the remaining flesh surrounding the pit, add the mango to the pan, and stir together. Continue to simmer, stirring every once in a while for 15 minutes.

Add the apples and 1¾ cups water and simmer for 20 minutes.

Add the sugar and simmer for 1 to 1½ hours. The chutney should be pulpy and thick but the mango slices still intact. Ladle into warm sterilized jars and seal.

CHICKEN SKEWERS WITH MANGO AND GINGER SAUCE

A recipe that brings back cherished memories of a very hot summer spent grape-picking in Bordeaux with my dear and, since lost, friend Richard Shaw. We ate a similar dish to this prepared by his mother, and I have been making a variation of it ever since. If you prefer, cook the skewers on the grill.

Serves 4

2 tablespoons peanut butter

1½ tablespoons olive oil

juice of 1 lemon

freshly ground black pepper

1½lb (750g) chicken thigh fillets, skinned and cut into chunks

3 large zucchini, cut into chunks

2 to 3 lemons, cut into chunks

24 fresh bay leaves

For the sauce

7 tablespoons olive oil

3 tablespoons soy sauce

1½ tablespoons rice wine vinegar

3 heaping tablespoons Mango Chutney (see page 29)

1 tablespoon sweet chili sauce

1 large garlic clove, peeled and crushed

2½in (6cm) piece of fresh ginger, peeled and grated

2 teaspoons superfine sugar

Put the peanut butter, olive oil, and lemon juice into a bowl with a good grinding of black pepper and mix together. Add the chicken and combine. Leave to marinate, covered, in the fridge for 2 to 3 hours.

Meanwhile, make the sauce. Put all the sauce ingredients into a food processor, adding 1 tablespoon hot water, and blend for a minute or two until you have a smooth sauce. Pour into a bowl and chill until required.

Soak 12 wooden skewers in water for 20 minutes. Then thread the chicken, zucchini, lemon, and bay leaves (folded in two) onto the skewers. Place the skewers onto a baking sheet and broil for about 15 minutes, turning once, or until the chicken is cooked.

Leave to rest for 5 minutes, then serve with new potatoes, salad, and the bowl of sauce to pass around.

Pineapple, Cilantro, and Lime Relish

This relish complements both fish and chicken really well and is a great alternative to the relishes you would normally see on the table at a barbecue. It has a slightly Asian kick, but actually works well with Cajun spices too.

Makes about 1 quart (1 liter)
Keeps for about 6 months

1 large ripe pineapple, peeled and
   cut into medium-sized chunks
2 red onions, peeled and chopped
2in (5cm) piece of fresh ginger, peeled and chopped
2 long red chili peppers, seeded and chopped
2 large garlic cloves, peeled and sliced
1 cup granulated sugar
2/3 cup white wine vinegar
juice of 3 limes
2 teaspoons fish sauce
1 teaspoon soy sauce
1 small bunch of cilantro, stems and
   leaves chopped but kept separate

Add all the ingredients except the cilantro to a large pan and gently bring to a boil. Simmer for 1 to 1½ hours, stirring occasionally, until most of the liquid has evaporated and the rest looks syrupy.

Stir in the cilantro, then immediately transfer to warm sterilized jars and seal.

ASIAN TUNA WITH PINEAPPLE RELISH

Years ago, I seasoned some tuna for a niçoise salad with a splash of soy sauce and lime and the results were truly amazing. The combination really wakes up the taste of the fish and also goes beautifully with a simple salad and some salsa. Try cooking the tuna on the grill once the sun starts shining.

Serves 4

4 thick fresh tuna steaks
1½ tablespoons soy sauce
juice of 1 lime
1 tablespoon extra virgin olive oil
freshly ground black pepper
dressed salad leaves and lime wedges, to serve
1 quart (1 liter) Pineapple, Cilantro, and Lime Relish
   (see left), or make a quick salsa with fresh pineapple,
   chopped chili pepper, lime juice, and fresh cilantro

Put the tuna steaks into a dish. In a small bowl, combine the soy sauce, lime juice, and olive oil with some freshly ground pepper and pour this mixture over the steaks. Leave out of the fridge to marinate for 30 minutes.

Heat a ridged grill pan until very hot and sear the tuna for 2 to 3 minutes on each side, or until cooked to your liking. (If, like me, you want to serve the tuna rare in the middle, remove the steaks from the heat while you can still see a line of pink around the middle of the outsides.)

Serve with the salad, lime wedges, and relish.

Chili Vodka

If you don't want the bother of sterilizing bottles, you could just buy a bottle of vodka and push the aromatics in. It won't keep as well, but if you're making it for a party, it won't last long anyway!

Makes 2 cups
Keeps for up to a year
2 green chili peppers, skins pricked
2 cups vodka

Put the chili peppers into a 2-cup bottle and fill with vodka. Leave for 3 to 4 days, then siphon off the flavored vodka into a clean sterilized glass bottle and seal.

Variation: Basil Vodka
Add 8 basil leaves to 2 cups vodka, then follow the instructions above.

Variation: Garlic Vodka
Peel and halve 2 large garlic cloves before adding them to 2 cups vodka, then follow the instructions above.

THE BEST BLOODY MARY

This recipe is based on one from Jarina and Brian Ahearn of the Wool Pack Inn in Northington, Hampshire, England, makers of the best Bloody Mary I have ever tasted— a fabulous Sunday morning wake-up in preparation for their heavenly roast beef. If you don't want to make three different flavored vodkas, use $2/3$ cup of basil vodka instead—it will work nearly as well.

Serves 6
¼ cup each Garlic, Basil, and Chili Vodka (see left)
¼ cup whiskey
¼ cup Sherry
¼ cup ginger wine
good dash of Worcestershire sauce
few drops of Tabasco sauce
pinch of celery salt
tomato juice, to top off
freshly ground black pepper
1 to 2 lemons, sliced

Put all the ingredients except the tomato juice, lemon slices, and black pepper into a large pitcher and stir well. Top with tomato juice and add black pepper to taste.

Run a lemon slice around the rims of 6 glasses and pour in the Bloody Mary mixture. Garnish each glass with a fresh slice of lemon and serve.

Mint and Apple Jelly

The addition of green food coloring is not something I would normally be in favor of but, in my mind, mint jelly really does need to be green and, without a little help, it looks distinctly unappealing!

Makes about 1 quart (1 liter)
Keeps for up to a year
3lb (1.3kg) cooking apples
3 lemons, thickly sliced
10 sprigs mint, plus 2oz (60g) mint leaves, chopped
about 5 cups granulated sugar
½ cup white wine vinegar
green food coloring (optional)

Cut the unpeeled, uncored apples into chunks and put them into a pan with the lemon slices, mint sprigs, and 1½ quarts (1¼ liters) water. Bring up to a boil, then simmer for about 40 minutes until collapsed. Pour into a jelly strainer, or a cheesecloth-lined sieve, and leave for 6 hours, or overnight, to strain.

Measure the liquid, pour into a pan, and bring to a boil. Weigh out 2¼ cups sugar for every 2 cups juice and add to the boiling liquid. Add the vinegar and stir over low heat. Once the sugar has dissolved, increase the heat and boil for 10 minutes before testing for a set.

Skim off any residue with a spoon or, if there is only a little, run a piece of paper towel over the surface to lift it off. Once the jelly has reached setting point, stir in the chopped mint and food coloring, if using.

Allow to cool for 15 minutes to keep the mint from floating to the surface, then divide the jelly between sterilized jars and seal.

Sage, Apple, and Cider Sauce

The sage in my garden is at its best at this time of year, while cooking apples are always around, so this recipe has slipped into spring rather than autumn. This is a great sauce to keep on hand to accompany Sunday brunch or perk up some midweek chops (see page 39).

Makes about 1 quart (1 liter)
Keeps for at least a year
2 tablespoons of butter
splash of olive oil
1 large onion, peeled and finely chopped
3lb (1.3kg) cooking apples, peeled, cored and cut into slices
¾ cup granulated sugar
20 small sage leaves, chopped
1⅓ cups hard cider

Preheat the oven to 300°F (150°C). Heat the butter and oil in a pan, add the onion, and cook gently for 5 to 6 minutes or until the onion has softened.

Add the apples to the pan and continue to cook, stirring, for another 5 minutes, before adding the sugar, chopped sage leaves, and cider. Increase the heat and simmer vigorously for 10 to 15 minutes, or until the apples are soft and some of the liquid has evaporated.

Lay a dish cloth or kitchen towel in the bottom of a roasting pan and put warm sterilized jars on top, spacing them well apart. Pour the sauce into the jars and rest the lids on top. Add water to the pan to a depth of about ¾in. Bake in the oven for 20 minutes, then seal the jars.

BAKED PORK CHOPS WITH CRISPY POTATOES AND SAGE AND APPLE SAUCE

A locally farmed pork chop with crispy crackling cannot be beat, and this recipe is a favorite. It's a great dish for dinner parties, too, as it all pretty much gets thrown into one pan and tossed in the oven—my kind of cooking!

Serves 6

6 bone-in pork chops
6 tablespoons olive oil
2 teaspoons Dijon mustard
zest and juice of 1 lemon
salt and freshly ground black pepper
3lb (1.5kg) new potatoes
2 tablespoons butter

1 cup Sage, Apple, and Vintage Cider Sauce (see page 36), or sweetened puréed apple cooked with 1 teaspoon chopped sage
3 tablespoons crème fraîche

Put the pork chops into a large dish. In a small bowl, mix 3 tablespoons of the oil with the mustard and lemon zest and a good squeeze of the juice. Season with salt and pepper, then pour the marinade over the chops, rubbing it in. Leave for 20 minutes to 2 hours, depending on the time available.

When ready to cook, preheat the oven to 425°F (220°C). Blanch the potatoes in boiling salted water for 7 to 8 minutes. Drain thoroughly, halve lengthwise, and transfer into a large roasting pan. Drizzle over the remaining 3 tablespoons olive oil and season with salt and pepper, then toss together. Roast for 20 to 25 minutes, or until light golden and beginning to crisp.

Once the potatoes have been roasting for about 15 minutes, heat the butter in a frying pan. Add the pork chops 3 at a time and cook for 2 to 3 minutes on each side, or until nicely browned. Set aside while you cook the others. Remove the potatoes from the oven after 20 to 25 minutes cooking time, toss them around in the pan, then top with the chops. (Don't discard the frying pan yet as you'll need to use all the buttery pork juices later.) Return the pan to the oven for another 15 minutes, or until the chops are cooked through.

Just before everything is ready, add a splash of water to the frying pan and bring to a boil, scraping the bottom of the pan with a wooden spoon. Add the Sage, Apple, and Vintage Cider Sauce and the crème fraîche and heat through, adding a little extra water to make it less thick. Season to taste and serve with the pork chops, accompanied by the crispy roast potatoes and some steamed buttered greens, if desired.

Pesto Sauce

This is the best pesto I have ever eaten—a recipe by my good friend, Italian cookbook author Anna del Conte, from her book *Amaretto, Apple Cake, and Artichokes*. If you are planning to freeze it, it's best to add the cheese once the sauce has been defrosted or it will lose a little of its flavor. Use a mortar and pestle if you want to make this the traditional way.

Makes about 1²/₃ cups
Store in the fridge for up to
4 weeks unopened, or freeze
2oz (60g) bunch of basil
3 garlic cloves, peeled
3 tablespoons pine nuts
good pinch of sea salt flakes
¹/₃ cup extra virgin olive oil, plus a little
   extra for pouring over the pesto in the jars
4 tablespoons grated Parmesan
4 tablespoons grated Pecorino

Remove the leaves from the basil stems. Put the basil leaves, garlic, pine nuts, and salt into a food processor and blend together, pouring the oil in a steady stream through the funnel. Alternatively, pound the dry ingredients together in a mortar using a pestle and gradually add the oil, scraping down the sides of the mortar occasionally.

Pour into a bowl and stir in the cheeses. Pour the pesto into sterilized jars and add a little oil on top to preserve. Store in the fridge.

GRILLED VEGETABLES WITH PESTO AND MOZZARELLA

Great with bread as a light lunch, served on a large platter, or as an appetizer.

Serves 6 as an appetizer or 4 for lunch
2 red bell peppers, seeded and cut into wide strips
1 eggplant, sliced into ¼in (7mm) slices
2 zucchini, sliced thinly on the diagonal
1 to 2 tablespoons extra virgin olive oil
sea salt and freshly ground black pepper
1 bunch of asparagus (if in season)
2 tablespoons Pesto Sauce (see left)
squeeze of lemon juice
1 to 2 tablespoons extra virgin olive oil
¾lb (375g) buffalo mozzarella, drained and torn into pieces
warm ciabatta, to serve

Brush the pepper, eggplant, and zucchini slices with oil, and season them with sea salt and black pepper. Grill in batches until charred on both sides and set aside in a dish. The peppers will need to be pressed down onto the grill and will take a few more minutes to soften.

Steam the asparagus for 2 to 3 minutes, or until tender, then cool immediately in a bowl of very cold water. Cut the spears in half, and leave all the vegetables to cool until you are ready to serve them.

Mix the pesto with the lemon juice and enough extra virgin olive oil to make a runny sauce. Season with pepper (and salt, if you feel it needs a little extra) and taste for sharpness, adding a little extra oil or lemon if needed.

Arrange the vegetables on a serving platter or individual plates and scatter mozzarella over the top. Drizzle with the dressing and serve with warm ciabatta.

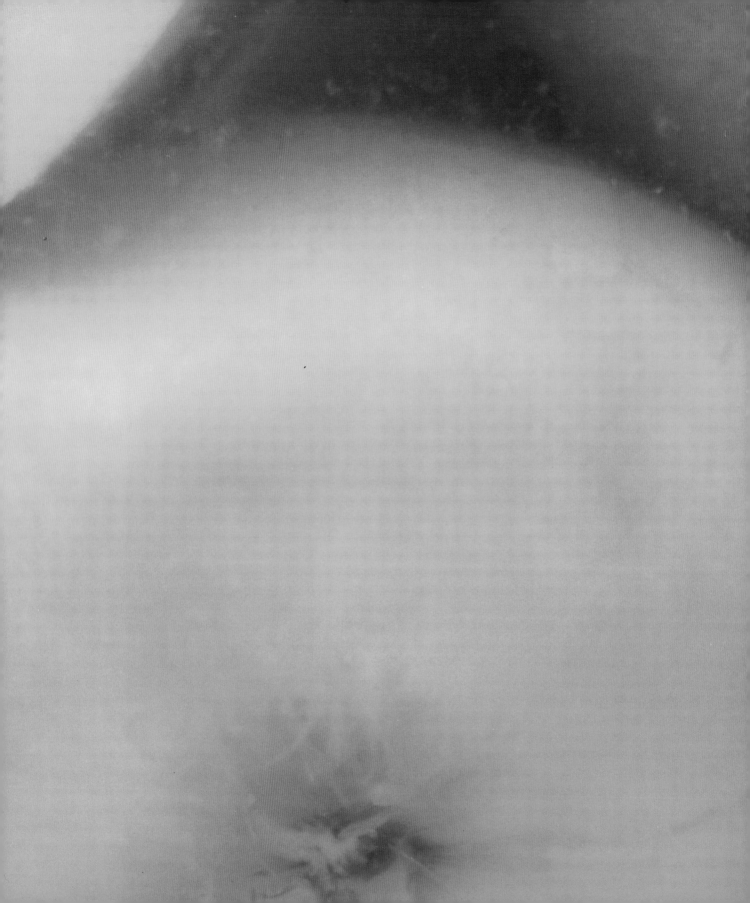

Summer

Pickled Beets

Those who grow beets always seem unable to grow it in small amounts—and there are frequently complaints from others in the family, who get sick of eating it boiled for weeks on end. Try this pickle recipe to keep the peace!

Makes 1¾ quarts (1.8 liters)
Keeps for up to 2 years

12 large beets, leaves and all but
    about 1¼in (3cm) of the stems removed
2 heaping tablespoons granulated sugar
1 cinnamon stick
8 cloves
½ teaspoon yellow mustard seeds
1 quart (1 liter) malt vinegar
½ teaspoon salt

Put the unpeeled, trimmed beets into a large pan of boiling salted water and cook for about 30 minutes, or until tender (pierce with a knife to test). Drain and leave to cool.

Meanwhile, put the sugar, spices, and vinegar into a pan with ½ teaspoon salt and slowly bring to a boil. Remove from the heat and let the liquid cool completely. Then reheat until warm when ready to bottle.

Wearing gloves, or with your hands in plastic bags to protect them, peel the beets, cut into good-sized chunks—about 2in (5cm)—and pack into warm sterilized jars. Pour in the warm vinegar, ensuring the beets are completely covered, and seal.

The pickled beets can be eaten after a day or so. It will be slightly milder tasting than if stored longer.

SMOKED TROUT AND BEET SALAD WITH SOUR CREAM DRESSING

This recipe is an homage to the wonderful county of Hampshire, England—home to rivers bursting with trout and watercress beds on every corner! The combination of peppery leaves with rich smoked trout and tangy beets is a winner. Add some warm sliced new potatoes if you want to make this salad even more substantial, and you could also replace the trout with smoked mackerel if you prefer.

Serves 4
For the dressing

3 tablespoons sour cream
1 tablespoon extra virgin olive oil
squeeze of lemon juice (about 2 teaspoons)
2 teaspoons creamed horseradish
1 heaping teaspoon chopped chives
salt, freshly ground black pepper, and sugar

For the salad

4 good handfuls of peppery salad leaves (I like the
    combination of watercress, spinach, and arugula)
½lb (225g) Pickled Beets (see left), drained and
    cut into smallish chunks
4 smoked trout fillets, skinned
8 radishes, sliced
1 bunch watercress, trimmed
1 tablespoon pumpkin seeds

In a bowl, mix the dressing ingredients together with about 2 teaspoons warm water and a pinch each of salt, pepper, and sugar.

Put the salad leaves on a serving platter or individual plates, then arrange the beets, trout, and radishes on top. Drizzle with the dressing, then scatter the watercress and pumpkin seeds over the top.

Onion, Port, and Thyme Marmalade

A jar of onion marmalade in the fridge is an essential ingredient for cooks. It's a great fix that adds a real depth of flavor to sauces and gravies, as well as accompanying cold meats.

Makes about 2½ cups
Keeps for at least a year

2lb (1kg) onions, peeled and halved
4 tablespoons olive oil
1 teaspoon sea salt
2 heaping teaspoons chopped fresh thyme leaves,
   or ¾ teaspoon dried thyme
½ cup dark brown sugar
3 tablespoons balsamic vinegar
3 tablespoons white wine vinegar
2 tablespoons Port
2 tablespoons redcurrant jelly
freshly ground black pepper

I find that putting the onions, quartered, through a slicer attachment on a food processor is the most stress-free way of slicing them for this recipe, as there are a lot to do by hand. If you prefer, just slice them thinly.

Heat the oil in a large pan, then add the onions, salt, and thyme and soften gently, stirring occasionally, for 35 to 40 minutes.

Once the onions are meltingly soft, add all the remaining ingredients, plus a good grind of black pepper, and bring slowly to a boil. Cook for another 10 minutes or so, stirring occasionally, until most of the liquid has evaporated. Spoon the mixture into warm sterilized jars and seal.

SAUSAGES, POTATOES, AND QUICK ONION GRAVY

Always a winner, especially if you have a butcher who makes great sausages. The onion gravy is also fabulous with a variety of other savory dishes.

Serves 2 to 3

6 pork and leek sausages (or other flavored sausages)
For the mash
½lb (225g) white potatoes
½lb (225g) sweet potatoes
¼ cup + 1 tablespoon milk
2 tablespoons of butter
pinch of grated nutmeg
For the gravy
3 tablespoons Onion, Port, and Thyme Marmalade (see left), or a store-bought onion marmalade
½ teaspoon English mustard
⅓ cup beef stock or beef consommé
freshly ground black pepper

Preheat the oven to 350°F (180°C). Place the sausages in a smallish roasting pan and cook for 25 to 30 minutes, turning once.

Peel all the potatoes, cut into large chunks, and cook in a pan of boiling salted water for 20 minutes, or until soft.

Meanwhile, make the gravy. Mix the onion marmalade, mustard, stock or consommé, and a good grinding of black pepper in a bowl and add to the sausages. Return the roasting pan to the oven for 10 to 15 minutes, or until the gravy is bubbling.

When the potatoes are done, drain them well. Warm the milk, butter, and grated nutmeg in the same pan, then add the potatoes and mash.

Serve the mashed potatoes with the sausages and onion gravy, accompanied by some buttered green beans if you wish.

Vanilla-poached Gooseberries

Gooseberries—or "goosgogs," as my grandfather used to call them—are a real favorite, but you don't necessarily want them turning up in every dessert while they are in season. My practical mother commented that people might as well just freeze their gooseberries because they keep so well but, if you don't have enough space in your freezer, you may prefer to poach them and store them in jars in the kitchen cabinet, ready to use. Gooseberries do lose a little color when poached, but they keep well and will happily perk up a pie or crumble all year round. The quantity of poaching liquid does seem to vary a little for some reason, but you can always try poaching some other fruit with what remains.

Makes about 1½ quarts (1.5 liters)
Keeps for up to 6 months
2 cups granulated sugar
1 vanilla bean, split
2½lb (1.2kg) gooseberries, trimmed

Use mason jars for this recipe, as they can withstand the temperature required for heat treatment. Preheat the oven to 300°F (150°C).

Put the sugar, vanilla bean, and 1⅔ cups water into a pan and heat gently until the sugar has dissolved, then increase the heat and boil for a minute.

Meanwhile, heat the jars in the oven for 5 minutes. (I find it's best to put about 1¾ quarts/1.8 liters worth of jars in to heat, as the yield can vary a little.)

Lay a dish cloth or kitchen towel in the bottom of a roasting pan and put the warm sterilized jars on top, spacing them well apart. Transfer the fruit to the jars, packing them really tightly, then pour in enough syrup to cover. Rest the lids on top without sealing. Add ¾in (2cm) boiling water to the pan and put into the oven for 20 to 25 minutes, or until the gooseberries are just tender. Remove the jars from the oven and seal immediately.

LIGHT GOOSEBERRY FOOL

This is a sort of fool, but slightly healthier than the normal version, in that you use Greek-style yogurt rather than heavy cream. (You'll therefore need to ensure that you make the custard quite thick, or the fool will end up too runny.) I prefer this lighter version, particularly if served after a meal. It's also, I'm told by my 12-year-old nephew, more chunky than normal fools. He suggested it could benefit from the addition of pieces of meringue. I imagine it would also be delicious frozen—although I haven't gotten around to trying that yet!

Serves 4
18oz (500ml) jar of *Vanilla-poached Gooseberries (see left), drained and syrup reserved, or poached fresh gooseberries, strained, with their syrupy juice reserved*
2 tablespoons custard powder (available in speciality stores or online)
2 to 3 teaspoons superfine sugar, if needed
2 cups Greek-style yogurt

First make the custard. Measure the gooseberry syrup into a glass pitcher; you should have 1 cup. If necessary, add a little water to make up the difference. Put the custard powder into a small pan with a little of the gooseberry syrup and stir together until smooth. Then stir in the rest of the syrup and heat gently, stirring with a whisk, until it reaches boiling point and has thickened. (Don't worry—it will look distinctly unappetizing at this stage!) Taste it for sweetness, adding a little superfine sugar if needed. Cool, covered with a layer a plastic wrap to prevent a skin from forming, then chill until required.

In a large bowl, mash the gooseberries slightly. Fold in the custard (beat it a little first until smooth to make it easier to mix in), then fold in the yogurt.

Pour the fool into glasses and chill for 30 minutes before serving, ideally, with some buttery cookies.

Gooseberry Jam

My mother has wonderful gooseberry bushes that provide masses of fruit in the early summer. She has a bed and breakfast, and I like to think that my requests for her to retest this jam twice for me have been greatly appreciated by her guests, who have eaten delicious homemade preserves with their toast! This jam also works perfectly well made with frozen fruit, but you might find it takes a little longer to reach a set.

Makes about 1½ quarts (1.5 liters)
Keeps for at least a year

2lb (1kg) fresh green gooseberries,
   slightly underripe, trimmed
5 cups granulated sugar

Put the gooseberries into a large pan with 1¼ cups water and gently simmer for 5 to 10 minutes, or until the gooseberries are beginning to soften. Add the sugar, stirring occasionally, until the sugar has dissolved and the gooseberries are softened.

Increase the heat and bring the jam to a rolling boil. Continue to boil for about 10 to 15 minutes, or until the jam has just reached setting point. Remove from the heat and leave for 10 minutes. Stir, then transfer the jam to warm sterilized jars and seal.

Strawberry and Rose Petal Syrup

I have to be honest—this began as an idea for a jelly but, after two rather impatient attempts at getting it right, I had a rare moment of clarity. I suddenly realized that a beautifully perfumed syrup is in fact far more versatile: it can be used to drizzle over ice cream, as an alternative to cassis for a summer cocktail, as a wonderful glaze for fresh strawberries, and as a ripple for cream-filled meringues (see page 56). It also makes a really lovely present to offer someone. If, however, you would prefer a jelly, just boil the liquid until setting point is reached, then transfer it to sterilized jars.

Makes 1 quart (1 liter)
Keeps for up to a year

2lb (1kg) strawberries
juice of 2 lemons
1 tablespoon rose water
2 cups granulated sugar per 2 cups juice
handful of rose petals
liquid or powdered pectin (optional): use according to package
    instructions if set is not achieved

Put the strawberries into a pan with 1 1/3 cups water and the lemon juice and simmer over medium heat until the strawberries have collapsed and softened. Mash using a potato masher, then transfer to a jelly bag and strain.

Measure the liquid and pour into a large pan. Add the rose water and 2 cups of sugar for every 2 cups of liquid, and stir over low heat until the sugar has dissolved.

The next stage is a tricky one to give exact timings for as it depends entirely on the strawberries you are using and how ripe they are. I have found, after various testings, that the easiest method is to bring the liquid to a rolling boil, then continue to boil for another 5 minutes. Remove from the heat and pour a little of the syrup onto a cold saucer. After 30 seconds in the fridge, it should feel thicker and look like a syrup, but should not wrinkle when you run your finger through it. If it is still too watery, heat it up again and boil for a few more minutes, then retest in the same way. It's best to be cautious: you want the end result to be a thickened but pourable syrup, so it must not reach setting point. Once the syrup has reached the right consistency, remove the pan from the heat and cool for 10 minutes.

Put 4 to 5 rose petals into the bottom of each of your warm, but not boiling hot, sterilized jars or bottles and pour in the warm syrup. Seal and cool completely.

BILLOWY MERINGUES WITH RIPPLED STRAWBERRY AND ROSE FILLING

My maternal grandmother made legendary meringues, which my mother and I have spent years attempting to perfect. The key is to cook them in a conventional rather than a convection oven, to use white rather than unrefined sugar and, most importantly, to be patient, adding the sugar a little at a time using a teaspoon. The resultant meringues really are worth waiting for! If you prefer, you can make smaller meringues and sandwich them together with the strawberry cream—just remember to reduce the cooking time slightly.

Serves 10
4 large egg whites, at room temperature
1¼ cups superfine sugar
6 tablespoons Strawberry and Rose Petal Syrup (see page 55)
2¾lb (1.3kg) strawberries, hulled and halved if large
1²⁄₃ cups heavy cream
rose petals, to decorate (optional)

First make the meringues. Preheat the oven to 225°F (110°C). Put the egg whites into a large clean china or glass bowl and, using a hand-held electric whisk, beat on the lowest speed for about 1 minute. Increase the speed one notch and keep whisking until the mixture is just stiff enough to stand in a peak when you lift the whisk out. Be careful not to overwhisk. Now, with the whisk at the next notch up in speed, add the sugar, a heaping teaspoon at a time, whisking for about 4 seconds between each addition.

Line 2 baking sheets with parchment paper. Spoon the meringue mixture in big dollops (about 2 teaspoons worth) onto the baking sheets, spacing the mounds well apart. You should have enough mixture for 10 meringues. Bake for 1 hour 20 minutes, or until the meringues are crisp and their bottoms sound hollow when tapped. Leave them to cool on their sheets and then transfer to an airtight container. They will keep for up to 2 weeks.

Mix 2 tablespoons of the syrup with the strawberries and leave to marinate for up to 4 hours. Softly whip the cream and gently stir in the remaining strawberry syrup until rippled. Leave in the fridge until you are ready to serve.

To serve, place a meringue and some strawberries onto each plate with a big dollop of the strawberry cream. Decorate with rose petals, if available.

Apricot Jam

This is a runny jam, with chunky bits of fruit and sweet honey-like aromas. A sort of cross between a jam and a compote, it reminds me of breakfasts in the garden on vacation in France.

Makes about 1½ quarts (1.5 liters)
Keeps for at least a year

3⅓lb (1.5kg) fresh apricots, not too soft
5 cups granulated sugar
juice of 2 lemons

Halve and pit the apricots, then cut in half again (or into smaller pieces if you prefer your jam less chunky). Put into a big bowl, then toss with the sugar and lemon juice. Leave the mixture to macerate in the bowl for 2 hours, which will give the fruit time to release its juices.

Transfer to a large pan and heat gently, stirring occasionally, until the sugar has dissolved and the apricots are just starting to soften. Increase the heat and bring the jam to a rolling boil. Continue to boil for 5 to 10 minutes, until the jam has just reached setting point. Remove from the heat and leave for 10 minutes. Stir, then transfer the jam to warm sterilized jars and seal.

APRICOT AND AMARETTO CRUMBLES

Adding a few drops of jam intensifies the flavor of the crumble enormously. The additional sugar is not essential; whether or not you need it will depend on personal taste and on how sweet and ripe your apricots are. If you want to make individual crumbles, you will need 6 x ½ cup ramekins. Alternatively, you can simply make the crumble in one large dish, allowing a few extra minutes of cooking time.

Serves 6
For the crumble

1⅓ cups all-purpose flour
5 tablespoons butter, chopped
½ cup light brown sugar plus 1 heaping
   tablespoon (optional) for the filling
⅓ cup toasted almond flakes

For the filling

10 to 11 fresh apricots, pitted and chopped
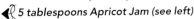 *5 tablespoons Apricot Jam (see left)*
1½ tablespoons amaretto

To serve

⅔ cup crème fraîche
1 to 2 tablespoons honey

Preheat the oven to 350°F (180°C). In a bowl, rub together the flour and butter until crumbly, then stir in the sugar and almonds.

Put the apricots into a separate bowl and stir in the jam, amaretto, and 3 tablespoons water. If your apricots are on the tart side, add extra sugar.

Divide the apricot filling between 6 ramekins (or put into an ovenproof dish) and top with the crumble mixture. Put the ramekins on a baking sheet and bake for 30 to 35 minutes, or until the fruit filling is bubbling and the top is golden.

Mix the crème fraîche with honey to your taste and chill. Serve with the crumbles.

Cherries in Brandy

I initially wondered whether or not this recipe was a bit old-fashioned, but as they say, the old ones are the best, and making the syrup lighter and less sugary makes the end result more appealing.

Makes about 1¾ quarts (1.8 liters)
Keeps for at least 6 months
1⅓ cups granulated sugar
1 cup brandy
2⅔lb (1.2kg) cherries

Use mason jars for this recipe, as they can withstand the temperature required for heat treatment. Preheat the oven to 300°F (150°C).

Put the sugar in a pan with 1½ cups water and heat gently until the sugar has dissolved. Bring to a boil, then turn off the heat and add the brandy.

Pack the cherries into sterilized mason jars and pour in enough syrup to cover. Lay a dish cloth or kitchen towel in the bottom of a roasting pan to prevent slippage and put the warm sterilized jars on top, spacing them well apart. Pour boiling water into the pan to a depth of about ¾in (2cm) and rest the lids on top of the jars, then put into the oven.

Bake for 30 minutes, remove the pan from the oven, and seal the jars with their lids.

Variation: Cherries in Spiced Rum
Make as above, replacing the brandy with 1 cup vanilla spiced rum.

CINNAMON FRENCH TOAST WITH CHERRIES

Wonderful for either dessert or brunch, the crisp brioche with syrupy cherries and cool ice cream is heaven sent!

Serves 2
5½oz (150g) Cherries in Brandy (see left), plus 1 cup of the liquor, or use poached and softened fresh cherries
2 tablespoons superfine sugar
good-quality vanilla ice cream, to serve
For the French toast
2 tablespoons milk
2 eggs
3 heaping teaspoons superfine sugar
2 pinches of cinnamon
4 slices of brioche
2 tablespoons butter, for cooking

Pit the cherries and set aside. Put the syrup and the 2 tablespoons of sugar into a pan and heat gently until the sugar has dissolved. Increase the heat and boil for 8 to 10 minutes, until the syrup has reduced to a thicker glossy sauce. Add the cherries and warm through.

To make the French toast, whisk together the milk, eggs, sugar, and cinnamon in a dish large enough to soak the bread. Add the brioche slices and turn over in the eggy mixture until well coated. Melt the butter in a frying pan and add the brioche. Cook for 2 to 3 minutes on each side or until deep golden.

Put the French toast onto plates, spoon over the cherries, and serve with a scoop of vanilla ice cream, drizzled with more cherry sauce.

Cherry Berry Jam

I think this is the tastiest of all the jams in the book—the combination of the different fruits is definitely greater than the sum of its parts. It is supposed to be a softer set jam, but if you prefer, you can keep it boiling for longer to reach a firmer set.

Makes about 1½ quarts (1.5 liters)

1¼lb (600g) cherries, pitted and halved

1lb (500g) strawberries, not too ripe, hulled and chopped into large chunks

½lb (225g) raspberries

juice of 2 lemons

5 cups granulated sugar

liquid or powdered pectin (optional): use according to package instructions if set is not achieved

Put all the ingredients into a bowl and stir together. Leave the mixture to macerate in a bowl for 2 hours, which will give the fruit time to release its juices.

Transfer to a large saucepan and gently bring to a simmer. Stir occasionally for the next 10 to 15 minutes to dissolve the sugar and begin to soften the fruits, then increase the heat to high and boil for 10 to 15 minutes, or until the jam has reached setting point.

Leave the jam to settle for 10 minutes before spooning it into warm sterilized jars and sealing.

Mixed Berry Jam

This jam offers a glimpse of summer days in a jar—bright and colorful and tasting as though the berries have just been harvested. It's great on toast but also provides a delicious way of brightening up a fruit tart or, as in the recipe on the right, enliven an ice cream. It is soft set, which I prefer, as it seems to taste fresher and is more versatile when fairly runny. If you have missed the blackcurrant season, simply increase the weight of the other fruits or substitute another favorite berry—although I think the blackcurrants add a wonderful tartness.

Makes about 1½ quarts (1.5 liters)
Keeps for at least a year

1lb (500g) strawberries, not too ripe, hulled and halved
¾lb (350g) blackcurrants
¾lb (350g) raspberries
juice of 2 lemons
juice of 1 orange
5 cups granulated sugar
liquid or powdered pectin (optional): use according to
    package instructions if set is not achieved

Put all the ingredients into a bowl and stir together. Leave the mixture to macerate in a bowl for 2 hours, which will give the fruit time to release its juices.

Transfer to a large saucepan and gently bring to a simmer. Stir occasionally for the next 10 to 15 minutes to dissolve the sugar and begin to soften the fruits, then increase the heat to high and boil for 10 to 15 minutes, or until the jam has reached setting point.

Leave the jam to settle for 10 minutes before spooning it into warm sterilized jars and sealing.

MIXED BERRY YOGURT ICE CREAM

My grandmother Sybil made quick ice cream using custard and jam. My father thinks she must have frozen it outside in the winter as this was years before people had freezers at home. This is my attempt at her ice cream, made with the addition of yogurt, for extra tang.

Makes 1½ quarts (1.5 liters)

2 cups creamy plain yogurt (can be low fat)
2 cups fresh thick custard
1½ cups Mixed Berry Jam (see left),
    or any tart red fruit jam that you like

In a bowl, mix together the yogurt, custard, and jam. Pour into freezer-proof container with a lid and freeze for about 1½ hours, or until the ice cream is partially frozen.

Transfer to a food processor and blend, then pour back into the container and freeze until ready. Serve in ice cream cones, if you wish.

Redcurrant Jelly

I have fond memories of selling plums and red and white currants as a child, at the bottom of our garden, to passing tourists visiting the local sites. I remember one particular car stopping and asking if white currants were nice and sweet and suitable for eating just as they were. "Oh yes," I said, fibbing my way to another 50 cents pocket money!

Makes about 1½ quarts (1.5 liters)
Keeps for up to a year
2lb (1kg) redcurrants, washed but kept on their stems
about 2½ cups granulated sugar

Put the redcurrants into a pan with 1⅔ cups water and cook for 20 to 30 minutes, or until the fruit is soft and has burst open to release its juice. Pour into a jelly bag and leave to strain through overnight.

Measure the strained liquid into a pitcher. Weigh out 2 cups sugar per 2 cups redcurrant juice and add both to a pan. Heat gently, stirring, until the sugar has dissolved, then increase the heat and bring to a rolling boil. Boil for 15 minutes then test for a set. Continue to cook until a set is achieved, then pour into warm sterilized jars and seal.

Variation: Redcurrant and Rosemary Jelly

Follow the recipe above, adding 2 tablespoons Port and 2 teaspoons very finely chopped fresh rosemary to the redcurrant juice at the same time as the sugar.

Cumberland Jelly

Easy to make, and probably my favorite of all things to serve with cold meats at Christmas time. I tend to make a double batch of redcurrant jelly up to the point of adding the sugar, then just turn half into Cumberland jelly.

Makes about 1½ quarts (1.5 liters)
Keeps for up to a year
2lb (1kg) redcurrants, washed but kept on their stem
½ cup Port
2 lemons, zest of both and juice of 1
2 large oranges, zest of both and juice of 1
1½ heaping teaspoons mustard powder
¾ teaspoon ground ginger
about 2½ cups granulated sugar

Put the redcurrants into a pan with 1⅔ cups water and cook for 20 to 30 minutes, or until the fruit is soft and has burst open to release its juice. Pour into a jelly bag and leave to strain through overnight.

Measure the strained liquid into a pitcher. Pour into a pan and add the Port, strained lemon and orange juice, zest, mustard powder, and ginger. Weigh out 2 cups sugar per 2 cups redcurrant juice and add to the pan.

Heat gently, stirring, until the sugar has dissolved, then increase the heat and bring to a rolling boil. Boil for 15 minutes, then test for a set. Continue to cook until a set is achieved, then pour into warm sterilized jars and seal.

CUMBERLAND HAM

I regularly cook a large ham, whether we have a big celebration or not. Although it an be a costly outlay, a good-sized piece of ham will provide many feasts and, more importantly, the leftovers are almost more delicious than the meal itself! There are endless tasty possibilities, including chicken and ham pot pie, pea and ham soup, and the ham on page 123.

Serves 10 to 12

1 x 9lb (4kg) boneless unsmoked ham
3 celery stalks, each cut into thirds
3 carrots , peeled and cut into large chunks
1 onion, peeled and quartered
small bunch of parsley
3 bay leaves
12 peppercorns

For the glaze

 *4 tablespoons Cumberland Jelly (see page 67)*
1½ tablespoons wholegrain mustard

Place the ham in a large pan and cover with cold water. Add the vegetables, herbs, and peppercorns, then cover with a lid and bring to a boil. Reduce the heat and very gently simmer, with the lid half on, for 2 hours and 20 minutes, then turn off the heat, remove the lid, and let the ham cool, in the liquid, in a cool place. Preheat the oven to 425°F (220°C).

Remove the ham from the liquid and place on a cutting board. (Reserve the ham stock.) Using a sharp knife, remove all the skin, leaving the fat in place. Score a criss-cross pattern through the fat. Transfer the ham to a roasting pan.

In a small bowl, mix the Cumberland Jelly with the mustard and smear half of it over the ham. Ladle enough of the ham stock into the roasting pan to cover the bottom and place in the oven. Bake for 30 to 40 minutes, or until the glaze has browned, smearing with the remaining glaze half way through the roasting time and topping off with more stock as it dries out.

If you are eating the ham hot, the stock remaining in the bottom of the pan can be served as extra juice (reheat a little more of the ham stock too, if necessary). Leave the cooked ham to stand for 15 minutes in a warm place before carving, or let cool completely.

Blackcurrant Jam

My great-grandmother Pom always made blackcurrant jam, and believed that a spoonful of jam, mixed with boiling water, was a sure-fire way to cure a cold. (I think she thought that strong Martinis and peppermints were medicinal, too, as she made sure she always had a good supply of these at all times and, consequently, lived until she was well into her 90s!) This recipe makes quite a large batch of jam. Feel free to halve the quantity, remembering to adjust the cooking times accordingly.

Makes about 3 quarts (3 liters)
Keeps for at least a year

4lb (1.8kg) blackcurrants, pulled from their stems and
   washed, but small flowery ends kept intact
9 cups granulated sugar

Put the blackcurrants into a large saucepan with 2 cups water and bring to a boil, then reduce the heat and simmer for 25 minutes or until softened.

Add the sugar and stir until gently dissolved, then increase the heat and bring to a rolling boil. Boil for around 5 to 8 minutes, then test for a set.

When the jam has reached setting point, remove from the heat and leave to cool for 30 minutes, stirring occasionally, before pouring into warm sterilized jars and sealing.

Tarragon Vinegar

Once you have this stored in your kitchen cabinet you will use it all the time, as unlike other herbs, tarragon isn't necessarily one that you will grow in your garden.

Makes 1²⁄₃ cups
Keeps for up to 6 months
3 tablespoons chopped fresh tarragon leaves
1²⁄₃ cups white wine vinegar

Combine the tarragon and vinegar in a sterilized mason jar. Seal and store for 3 weeks.

Strain the vinegar before decanting it into another sterilized bottle.

Variation: Basil Vinegar

Follow the instructions above, using 4 tablespoons chopped fresh basil leaves in place of the tarragon.

ROAST CHICKEN AND SHRIMP SALAD WITH TARRAGON SAUCE

A slightly more sophisticated alternative to chicken salad, and perfect for family parties.

Serves 4 to 6
1 x 3½lb (1.6kg) chicken
salt and freshly ground black pepper
½ lemon
olive oil for drizzling
9oz (250g) cooked and peeled shrimp
1oz (30g) toasted almond flakes
For the dressing
1 large egg yolk
1 heaping teaspoon wholegrain mustard
1 teaspoon superfine sugar
⅓ cup mild olive oil
1½ tablespoons Tarragon Vinegar (see left)
   or 1½ tablespoons white wine vinegar
4 tablespoons crème fraîche
1 heaping tablespoon fresh tarragon, chopped

Preheat the oven to 425°F (220°C). Season the chicken, place in a roasting pan, stick half a lemon into the cavity, and drizzle with olive oil. Roast for 15 minutes.

Reduce the oven temperature to 350°F (180°C), baste the chicken with any juices, and continue to cook for another 50 minutes, or until the juices in the thigh run clear when pierced with a knife or skewer. Cool in the pan, then remove the flesh from the carcass and cut into bite-sized pieces. Chill until required.

Make the dressing: put the egg yolk into a bowl with 2 teaspoons warm water, the mustard, sugar, salt, and pepper. Whisk together, then gradually add the oil in a fine drizzle, whisking until fairly thick. Add the vinegar, in two parts, whisking between each, then the crème fraiche and tarragon. Stir, taste, and check the seasoning. Stir in the chicken and shrimp and refrigerate for up to 2 hours.

Transfer to a bowl, sprinkle with the almonds, and serve with crunchy lettuce leaves.

Green Bean Relish

An easy-to-make relish that tastes better the longer you leave it to mature—I'd recommend you wait a minimum of 4 weeks before digging in. It makes a great accompaniment to cold roast pork or lamb.

Makes 2½ quarts (2.5 liters)
Keeps for at least 6 months

2 large onions, peeled and finely chopped
1 large garlic clove, peeled and sliced
1 red chili pepper, seeded and finely chopped
1 quart (1 liter) malt vinegar
2½ cups light brown sugar
1 heaping teaspoon yellow mustard seeds
1 teaspoon flaky sea salt
2lb (1kg) green beans, trimmed and sliced on the diagonal into ¾in (2cm) pieces
2 tablespoons cornstarch
2 teaspoons ground turmeric
1 teaspoon English mustard powder

Put the onions, garlic, chili pepper, vinegar, sugar, mustard seeds, and salt into a large pan and bring to a boil. Simmer gently for 20 minutes. Bring back to a boil, then add the green beans and boil for 15 minutes.

Meanwhile, in a small bowl, mix together the cornstarch, turmeric, and mustard powder with a dash of water to make a runny paste. Add to the pan, stirring until the paste has been incorporated. Simmer for a final 15 minutes.

Ladle into warm sterilized jars and seal. Leave for 4 weeks before trying.

Corn Relish

This is a world away from the over-sweet syrupy type available in the supermarket. Try it with barbecued burgers or chicken.

Makes 1½ quarts (1.5 liters)
Keeps for at least a year

5 fresh ears corn on the cob
2 peppers (any color), seeded and chopped
3 celery stalks, finely chopped
1 onion, finely chopped
2 garlic cloves, finely chopped
1 to 2 red chili peppers (depending on preference), seeded and finely chopped
1¾ cups granulated sugar
1½ cups cider vinegar
sea salt
⅓ cup all-purpose flour
1 teaspoon yellow mustard seeds
¾ teaspoon ground turmeric
½ teaspoon celery seeds

Bring a large pan of water to a boil. Add the corn, bring back to a boil, then cook for 4 minutes. Remove from the heat and pour ⅔ cup of the cooking water into a pitcher, discarding the remainder and draining the cobs. Leave them to cool slightly.

Using a large, very sharp knife, carefully cut down the corn cobs, removing the corn niblets from their husks. (I find it easiest to hold the cob up on a cutting board and, very carefully, run the knife down each side, working my way around.)

Put the corn niblets, peppers, celery, onion, garlic, and chili peppers into the pan and add the sugar, vinegar, reserved cooking water, and a sprinkle of sea salt. Bring to a boil, stirring occasionally, and leave to bubble away for 10 minutes.

Meanwhile, mix the flour, mustard seeds, turmeric, and celery seeds together in a small bowl, then gradually add water to mix to a smooth pourable consistency—similar to heavy cream. Add to the pan, stirring while you pour. Simmer for another 15 minutes before transferring into warm sterilized jars.

Peaches Poached in Muscat

Serve either warm or chilled with vanilla ice cream or a dollop of mascarpone mixed with vanilla seeds and a dash of sugar—bliss! You can poach the peaches and serve them right from the pan if you like. Just simmer in the poaching liquid until tender. Substitute the peaches for nectarines if you prefer.

For 7 to 8 poached peaches
Keeps for 6 months
12oz (375ml) bottle of Muscat wine
1¼ cups granulated sugar
7 to 8 peaches

Preheat the oven to 325°F (160°C). Put the Muscat, sugar, and ¾ cup water into a pan, bring to a boil, and simmer for 10 minutes.

Meanwhile, slice a cross on the bottom of each peach and add to the poaching liquid. Leave for about 2 minutes, before removing with a slotted spoon and removing their skins.

Pack the peaches tightly into a warm sterilized jar and pour in the syrup. Lay a dish cloth or kitchen towel in the bottom of a roasting pan and put the jar on top. Add water to the pan to a depth of about ¾in (2cm). Bake for 30 minutes, then remove from the oven and seal the jar.

HEALTHIER PEACH AND NECTARINE BRÛLÉE

I'm reluctant to say this is anything like crème brûlée, as the only similarity is the crunchy top. It is yummy, though, and a lot more refreshing than the traditional kind, so ideal for a lunchtime dessert or after a heavy meal. You can use any chopped-up raw fruit in the bottom—I've used raw ripe summer fruits and poached plums with great success. You can also make this even healthier by using low-fat crème fraîche, but it might produce a slightly runnier top, so stick the chilled dish in the freezer for about 20 minutes before attempting the brûlée. I recommend using a blow torch for the brûlée, if you have one, as it's definitely more successful, but a powerful broiler will do the trick if you follow the suggestions below.

Serves 6 to 8
8 Peaches Poached in Muscat (see left), plus 5 tablespoons of their syrup, or 8 raw ripe peaches, peeled (see right-hand method)
14oz (400g) raspberries
1⅔ cups Greek-style yogurt
1⅔ cups crème fraîche
seeds from 1 vanilla bean, or 1 teaspoon vanilla extract
1 heaping tablespoon superfine sugar, plus about ¾ cup for the top

Cut the peaches into chunks and place in the bottom of a 4 to 6in (10–13cm)-deep ovenproof dish or 6 ramekins. Scatter the raspberries on top and drizzle with the syrup.

Mix the yogurt and crème fraîche together with the vanilla and 1 heaping tablespoon sugar and spoon over the fruit. Chill in the fridge for 2 hours or until required.

Sprinkle ¾ cup sugar over the top in a thick layer, then use a blowtorch to melt and caramelize the sugar. Alternatively, preheat the broiler, sit the dish or ramekins in a roasting pan of ice-cold water (to keep the dish from getting too hot underneath), and broil the top as close to the heat as you can.

Leave to cool for a few minutes until the topping is hard, then serve.

Peach and Nectarine Chutney

This chunky chutney is packed with fruit and is especially good served with cold or hot roast ham and new potatoes. Use all peaches or all nectarines if you prefer.

Makes about 3 cups
Keeps for at least a year

1 large onion, peeled and chopped
2 garlic cloves, chopped
1 to 2 red chili peppers, seeded and chopped
   (add the extra if you want more of a kick)
1 teaspoon ground ginger
½ teaspoon black mustard seeds
½ teaspoon yellow mustard seeds
1¼ cups cider vinegar
1½ cups light brown sugar
5 nectarines
5 peaches
juice of 1 lime

Put the onion, garlic, chili pepper, ginger, mustard seeds, and vinegar into a large pan, bring to a boil, then reduce the heat and simmer for 15 minutes. Stir in the sugar and cook for another 15 minutes.

Meanwhile, use a knife to slice a cross on the bottom of each fruit and put into a large bowl. Cover with freshly boiled water and leave for about 2 minutes, then drain, rinse with cold water, and remove their skins.

Cut the fruit into segments and add half to the pan. Simmer for 40 minutes, stirring occasionally, then add the remaining pieces of fruit and cook for a final 10 minutes.

Stir in the lime juice, pour the relish into warm sterilized jars, and seal.

Sweet Shallots in Balsamic Vinegar

I find it a bit hard to find pickling onions—hence the shallots—but feel free to swap. These pack a punch, and taste great on a sandwich of leftover meats. I've given a ranged weight of onions because the amount you can pack in will depend on the size of the jars and onions you use.

Makes 2 quarts (2 liters)
Keeps for 2 years

2½ to 3lb (1.2–1.4kg) small sweet or regular shallots
    or pickling onions
⅔ cup kosher salt
½ cup dark brown sugar
7 cloves
½ teaspoon crushed red pepper flakes
1¼ cups balsamic vinegar
1¼ cups good-quality red wine vinegar
fresh bay leaves (1 per jar)

Trim the shallots or pickling onions using a small sharp knife, then place in a bowl and cover with boiling water. Leave for 5 minutes, then drain and cover with cold water. Drain again and, using the knife, remove the skins.

Put the salt into a large glass bowl and pour in 1⅔ cups boiling water. Stir to dissolve the salt, then add another 1 quart (1 liter) cold water and the onions. In a pitcher, combine the sugar, cloves, and crushed red pepper flakes with the vinegars and 1 cup water. Leave the contents of both containers to marinate overnight.

After 12 hours or so, drain the onions and rinse thoroughly in cold water. Meanwhile, sterilize your jars in the oven. Pour the vinegar mixture into a pan and warm through gently, but don't boil.

Tightly pack the onions into the warm jars and pour in the warm vinegar. Add a bay leaf to each jar. The onions need to be completely covered with vinegar, so top off the jars with a little extra if necessary. Seal and store for 6 weeks before using.

COQ AU VIN

If you prefer, you can woo your guests by calling this retro favorite "Baked Chicken with Pancetta, Red Wine, and Balsamic Shallots" instead. Either way, it's ideal for a warm and cozy dinner party.

Serves 6

1 bottle of red wine
2 garlic cloves, sliced
3 bay leaves
2 teaspoons fresh thyme leaves
dash of olive oil
salt and freshly ground black pepper
6 chicken thighs and 6 drumsticks, skin on
3oz (75g) pancetta cubes
3 celery stalks, sliced
2 heaping tablespoons all-purpose flour
2 cups chicken stock, ideally fresh (store-bought is fine)
9 Sweet Shallots in Balsamic Vinegar (see left),
    drained and halved
9oz (250g) button mushrooms, quartered

Preheat the oven to 300°F (150°C). Pour the wine into an flameproof lidded casserole and add the garlic, bay leaves, and thyme. Bring to a boil, reduce by one third, then reduce the heat until the wine is gently simmering.

Meanwhile, heat a frying pan until hot and add the oil. Season the chicken pieces and cook in batches until brown all over. Transfer the chicken to the casserole.

Add the pancetta and celery to the frying pan and cook for 5 minutes, then add the flour and stir to combine. Gradually add the chicken stock and bring to a boil, then pour into the casserole.

Add the pickled shallots to the casserole and season with plenty of salt and black pepper. Bring back to a boil, then cover with the lid and transfer to the oven.

After 30 minutes, remove the casserole from the oven and stir in the mushrooms. Re-cover and return to the oven to cook for another 10 minutes.

If you prefer a more concentrated sauce, transfer the chicken and vegetables to a dish and rapidly boil the gravy on the stove for another 5 minutes or so. Taste for seasoning and serve with rice or mashed potatoes.

Lavender Sugar

You either love the taste of lavender or hate it. Don't use too much, or it will overpower whatever you are adding it to. Flavored sugars are great fun, particularly if you make and use them when cooking with children. They also look stunning when given as presents.

Makes ¾ cup

10 lavender flower heads
¾ cup superfine sugar

Combine the flower heads and sugar in a jar and leave to infuse for 3 days, shaking every day. Remove the flowers, then simply store the sugar until ready to use.

Vanilla Sugar

Often you will use just vanilla seeds in a recipe—but don't discard the beans as they can be used to make fantastic vanilla sugar.

Makes 1 cup

1 vanilla bean, whole or seeded
1 cup superfine sugar

Put the sugar and vanilla bean into a food processor and blend until thoroughly combined. Transfer to a jar and seal until ready to use.

LAVENDER PANNA COTTA

Panna cotta works well infused with many different flavors—the scraped seeds of a vanilla bean, a dash of espresso coffee, or jasmine tea are among my favorite additions. I think the key is to be subtle, though: add the flavoring a little at a time until you can detect just the merest hint.

Serves 6

2 cups heavy cream

1⅓ cups whole milk

 ¾ cup Lavender Sugar (see page 82)

4½ sheets of gelatin (each sheet measuring about 4 x 3in /11 x 7cm)

6 fresh lavender sprigs, to serve

Heat the cream, milk, and sugar in a saucepan gently until the sugar has dissolved and the liquid is piping hot, but not boiling.

Meanwhile, soak the gelatin sheets in a bowl of cold water for 5 minutes, until they have softened. Add the drained gelatin to the liquid and stir until completely melted. Pour into 6 individual large ramekins. Leave to cool, then chill for 4 to 6 hours.

When you are ready to serve the panna cottas, dip each ramekin into a bowl of boiling water for a couple of seconds, then turn them onto plates. Serve with a lavender sprig on top of each.

Strawberry Conserve Spiked with Orange

Strawberry jam can be a little tricky with regard to timings, and sometimes takes longer to set. Be patient, and just continue to test until you are happy that a setting point has been reached.

Makes about 1½ quarts (1.5 liters)
Keeps for at least a year

2lb (1kg) strawberries, not too ripe, hulled and halved

juice of 2 large lemons

zest of 2 oranges

5 cups granulated sugar

liquid or powdered pectin (optional): use according to
   package instructions if set is not achieved

Put all the ingredients into a bowl and stir to combine. Leave the mixture to macerate for 2 hours, which will give the fruit time to release its juices.

Transfer to a large saucepan and stir over low heat for about 10 minutes until the sugar has dissolved. Then increase the heat and bring to a rolling boil. Continue to boil for about 10 minutes, or until the jam reaches setting point.

Leave to cool for 15 minutes, then transfer the jam to warm sterilized jars and seal.

Autumn

Nearly My Grandmother's Green Tomato Chutney

Everyone on my father's side of the family remembers my grandmother Sybil's incredible green tomato chutney. I'm sure it was invented purely as a way to use up all the unripe tomatoes, as my grandparents were sticklers for not wasting anything. Sadly, the recipe for the chutney, as well as many others, disappeared after Sybil died. This nearly-but-not-quite version is the result of many conversations with various family members, as well as a distant memory of tasting the chutney myself. We think we can remember all the components—and which ingredients definitely wouldn't have been included due to their unavailability all those years ago—so here goes! Let's hope my grandmother isn't turning in her grave!

Makes about 1¾ quarts (1.7 liters)
Keeps for at least a year

2lb (1kg) green tomatoes, quartered

1lb (500g) onions, peeled and cut into wedges

1lb (500g) cooking apples, peeled, cored, and cut into quarters

1½ cups golden raisins

3 garlic cloves, peeled and crushed

2 teaspoons yellow mustard seeds

1½ teaspoons ground ginger

1 teaspoon cayenne pepper

1 heaping teaspoon sea salt flakes

½ teaspoon allspice

2 cups malt vinegar

2 cups dark brown sugar

In a food processor, process the tomatoes, onions, and apples in batches until they are pulpy, but still a bit chunky. Add all the remaining ingredients except for the brown sugar, stir, and bring to a boil. Reduce the heat and simmer for 1 hour, stirring occasionally.

Add the brown sugar and stir well, then leave to simmer, stirring every 15 minutes, for another 1 hour, or until the mixture has lost most of its water and leaves a trail when you pull a wooden spoon through it. (Timings vary from one batch to another—just keep checking and giving it a stir.)

Using a funnel and a ladle, spoon the hot chutney into warm sterilized jars and seal.

Late Raspberry Jam

I'm always late for everything, but I do feel in this case, waiting until late summer to make your raspberry jam is worth it. Try to find the plumpest, juiciest raspberries you can—they will be full of flavor.

Makes about 1½ quarts (1.5 liters)
Keeps for at least a year
2½lb (1.2kg) raspberries
juice of 2 lemons
5 cups granulated sugar

Put all the ingredients into a bowl and stir. Leave the mixture to macerate for 2 hours, which will give the fruit time to release its juices.

Transfer to a pan and stir over low heat until the sugar has dissolved, then increase the heat to bring to a rolling boil and cook for 5 to 10 minutes or until the jam reaches setting point.

Transfer the jam to warm sterilized jars and seal.

Variation: Raspberry and Kirsch Jam

Make the jam as above, stirring in 2 to 3 tablespoons Kirsch (or to taste) to the jam just after setting point has been reached.

RASPBERRY QUEEN

A favorite dessert of mine, which I love made with either raspberry or apricot jam. It is more practical to make it in one large dish, but if you like you could use 6 ramekins—just remember to reduce cooking times. How much jam you smother over is up to you—if you don't have such a sweet tooth, you might prefer a smaller amount than I've used here.

Serves 6
2 cups whole milk
2 tablespoons butter
1½ cups fresh bread crumbs, made using white,
   day-old bread with the crusts removed
¼ cup superfine sugar, plus ¼ cup for the meringue
zest of 1 large lemon
3 large eggs, separated
2 tablespoons Late Raspberry Jam (see left)
half-and-half, to serve

Preheat the oven to 350°F (180°C). Heat the milk and butter in a pan until the butter has melted and the liquid is hot, then turn off the heat and stir in the bread crumbs, sugar, and lemon zest. Leave to swell for 15 minutes, then beat in the egg yolks.

Pour the mixture evenly into a large ovenproof dish measuring 8 x 10in (26 x 20cm) with a depth of about 2in (5cm). Bake for 25 to 30 minutes or until set. (You can make the recipe up to this point an hour or two in advance if you like.)

Gently warm the jam in a pan to loosen it, then spread evenly over the surface. Whisk the egg whites until they form peaks, then keep whisking while you gradually add all but 2 teaspoons of the sugar. Spoon the meringue mixture on top of the dish and sprinkle with the remaining sugar. Bake in the center of the oven for 15 to 20 minutes or until golden.

Serve with half-and-half to pour over the top.

Raspberrycello

My cousin-in-law Tania made the inspired suggestion of using the leftover vodka-spiked raspberries in the bottom of a crème brûlée—I cannot tell you how delicious it is and, of course, there's no waste. This liqueur is a stunning pink and I'm sure it would make any cocktail a fabulous hit. You can replace the vodka with gin if you prefer.

Makes about 1 quart (1 liter)
Keeps for at least a year
½lb (225g) raspberries
25oz (750ml) vodka
1 cup granulated sugar

Put the raspberries into a large mason jar with the vodka and sugar. Seal, then leave to infuse for 2 weeks, inverting or shaking the jar every few days to redistribute the fruit and sugar.

Pour through a strainer into a pitcher, discarding or eating the raspberries. Taste for sweetness, adding more sugar to taste if necessary, then transfer into a clean bottle. Store in the freezer.

Variation: Limoncello

Remove the zest from 6 lemons and squeeze the juice from 2. Add to a large mason jar with 25oz (750ml) vodka and seal. Leave for about a week, inverting or shaking the jar every couple of days.

In a pan, heat 2 cups water with 2 cups sugar until dissolved. Leave to cool. Stir the sugar mixture into the vodka mixture and leave for another 10 days. Strain into bottles and keep in the freezer.

RASPBERRY VODKA SORBET

This delicious sorbet works equally well if it's made using an ice cream machine.

Serves 6 to 8
1¼ cups granulated sugar
1 cup lemon juice (about 3 to 4 large lemons)
◄ *1 cup Raspberrycello (see left)*

Bring the sugar and 1⅔ cups water slowly to a boil. Once the sugar has dissolved, stir in the lemon juice and Raspberrycello and cool.

Pour into a plastic container (or into an ice-cream maker) and freeze for 2½ hours or until half frozen. Break up any ice crystals using the back of a fork and return it to the freezer for another 4 to 5 hours.

Scoop the sorbet into glasses and serve, pouring in a little more of the liqueur if you wish.

Holy Sloe or Peach Gin

This recipe was very kindly passed on to me by the Reverend Kevin Mentzel, who I bumped into one day at a farmer's market. I have tweaked it slightly, making it a little sweeter for our tastes, and incorporated my husband's fantastic trick of "pricking" the frozen sloes using a cheese grater, which saves having to wait for the first frost and hours of mind-numbing pricking with a needle. You can substitute the gin for vodka if you prefer.

As sloes are very hard to find in North America, it is best to substitute with peaches instead. I have left the sloe recipe in for interest, and follow the same directions when using peaches, only halve the quantity of sugar as peaches have more natural sweetness than sloes.

Makes about 2 quarts (2 liters)
Keeps for at least 2 years

2½lb (1.2kg) sloes or peaches, frozen
3 cups granulated sugar (1½ cups if using peaches)
1½ quarts (1.5 liters) gin

Put the frozen sloes or peaches onto a large sheet and run the spiky, zesting side of a cheese grater over them, making sure that each sloe has been nicked.

Transfer the sloes to large sterilized mason jars, then pour in the sugar and finally the gin. Seal and shake to distribute the fruit.

Shake the jars once a day for the next week, then leave to mature for at least 3 months. Strain the gin into clean bottles, discarding the sloes/peaches.

Variation: Almond-infused Sloe Gin

Add 3 whole, unblanched almonds to the above recipe when preparing.

SLOE GIN FIZZ

This is an absolute favorite in my family—especially at Christmas time, when the sloe gin from that season should be just about ready to drink. The color is extremely festive too and can look stunning if topped with a couple of raspberries or pomegranate seeds.

Serves 6

12 teaspoons Holy Sloe or Peach Gin (see left)
12 to 18 raspberries or blueberries
1 bottle of Champagne or sparkling wine

Put 2 teaspoons sloe gin and 2 to 3 raspberries or blueberries in the bottom of each of 6 Champagne flutes. Top off with the Champagne or sparkling wine and serve immediately.

Plum and Blueberry Jam

The blueberries are not essential, but as they are my son's favorite and are packed with superfood goodness, they have found themselves added to the pot! They also add a wonderful purple hue to this jam.

Makes about 3 quarts (3 liters)
Keeps for at least a year
5½lb (2.5kg) ripe plums, pitted and chopped
   into bite-sized pieces
½lb (250g) blueberries
juice of 4 lemons
10 cups granulated sugar

Stir all the ingredients together in a bowl. Leave the mixture to macerate in the bowl for 2 hours, which will give the fruit time to release its juices.

Transfer the fruit to a pan and cook gently, until the plums have wrinkled and softened a little and the mixture has begun to rise in the pan. Increase the heat and boil for another 15 to 20 minutes, or until the jam has reached setting point.

Remove the pan from the heat and leave to cool for 10 minutes, then pour the jam into sterilized jars and seal.

PLUM, BLUEBERRY, AND ALMOND TART

This is a really easy recipe and it looks stunning. Serve it with chilled crème fraîche to balance the sweetness of the tart.

18oz (500g) block of frozen, all-butter puff pastry, defrosted
flour, for rolling pastry
millk, for brushing pastry
9oz (250g) block of white marzipan
¾lb (400g) plums, halved and pitted
2 tablespoons butter
¾ cup blueberries
**4 tablespoons Plum and Blueberry Jam (see page 99),
   or another berry jam**
2 tablespoons toasted almond flakes

Preheat the oven to 400°F (200°C). Roll out the pastry on a floured surface until it forms a rectangle measuring about 11in x 14in (29 x 37cm). Trim a ¾in (2cm) wide strip from all the edges and reserve. Place the pastry rectangle onto a baking sheet. Brush the edges with milk, then stick the strips all around the outside of the rectangle, trimming as necessary. Prick the bottom of the pastry with a fork.

Roll out the marzipan very thinly, then place it onto the pastry rectangle and, using both hands, pull it so that it sits inside the pastry, scrunching it up a little so that it looks like an unmade bed. Scatter the plum halves over the top, cut-side up, and dot them with the butter. Scatter with the blueberries. (If you wish, you can make the tart up to this stage and keep it in the fridge overnight).

Warm the jam with 3 tablespoons water to make it a little runnier, then drizzle half over the fruit. Scatter with the almonds and brush the exposed pastry edges with a little milk. Bake in the oven for 20 minutes.

Remove the tart from the oven, drizzle with the remaining jam, and return it to the oven for another 10 to 15 minutes, or until the pastry is golden and the plums are tender. Serve warm or cold with crème fraîche.

Gardener's Windfall Chutney

This recipe is ideal for the novice chutney maker as, having prepared the apples and onion, you simply throw everything into one big pot and let it simmer away. It also calls for few non-pantry ingredients, so it's perfect for those times when you come in from the garden and suddenly have the urge to create something using the produce you've harvested. Feel free to halve the quantities if preferred. One word of warning: be careful when stirring the hot chutney—it may be just trembling on the surface, but it can erupt like a volcano when you dig deeper. I find turning off the heat briefly helps...and wear an apron!

Makes about 3 quarts (3 liters)
Keeps for at least a year

3¼lb (1.5kg) fallen cooking apples, peeled, cored, and sliced

1 onion, peeled and chopped

4 x 14oz (398ml) cans of chopped tomatoes

1⅓ cups golden raisins

3¾ cups granulated sugar

2 teaspoons curry powder

2 teaspoons ground ginger

1½ heaping teaspoons salt

2 cups malt vinegar

Put all the ingredients into a very large pan (or divide between two slightly smaller ones). Cook over medium heat, stirring occasionally, for about 2½ hours, or until the mixture thickens and starts to become sticky. As the mixture cooks, the liquid will rise to the surface, with the chutney thickening at the bottom of the pan. Continue to stir every so often until the liquid has reduced to the point that it feels and looks less like a sauce and has formed the consistency of a chutney, then ladle or pour it into warm sterilized jars and seal.

The chutney can be eaten as soon as it is cool, unlike others, which need to be left to mature. Just be sure that your first taste of it is with some fresh white bread and really strong Cheddar. The combination is wonderful!

Variation: Feisty Windfall Chutney

Add 3 large mild red chili peppers, seeded and chopped, to the pot and mix well with the rest of the ingredients. Follow the recipe above.

SAUSAGE AND CHUTNEY
PICNIC PUFFS

These freeze beautifully and can be warmed and packed in aluminum foil
as a welcome addition to the usual cold picnic fare.

Makes 24

all-purpose flour, for dusting

15oz (425g) frozen ready-rolled puff pastry, defrosted

1 egg, beaten

4 tablespoons Gardener's Windfall Chutney (see page 105)

6 good-quality thick sausages

sesame seeds, for sprinkling

Preheat the oven to 400°F (200°C). On a floured surface roll out one of the pastry
rectangles to form a square.

Cut the pastry square in half and brush the edges of both rectangles with
beaten egg. Using a spoon, spread the chutney fairly thinly over the two pastry
pieces so that it nearly reaches to the edges. (Don't go too crazy with it or you'll
end up with a sticky baking sheet!)

Take three sausages from the pack and squeeze the meat from their skins.
Using the palms of your hands, roll each out into a thinner sausage. Lay the
meat lengthwise along the center of both rectangles of pastry (you'll need
to divide the third sausage between them).

Taking the long edge of each pastry rectangle, roll the pastry over the
meat to make two long sausage rolls. Brush with beaten egg and cut each roll
into six. Sprinkle with sesame seeds and place onto a non-stick baking sheet.

Repeat the same process with the second pastry rectangle and remaining
three sausages.

Bake both sheets in the center of the oven for about 20 to 25 minutes,
or until the pastry is golden brown. Remove the sausage rolls to a wire rack
to cool.

Vanilla Poached Pears

I'm not a huge fan of heavy pears in red wine, but was inspired to try using pear cider having watched a chef using it in a jelly, which he served with elderflower ice cream.

Makes about 2 quarts (2 liters)
Keeps for 6 months
1 quart (1 liter) alcoholic pear cider
2 cups granulated sugar
1 vanilla bean, split lengthwise
2 strips of lemon zest
3 tablespoons honey
4lb (1.8kg) underripe pears

Use mason jars for this recipe, as they can withstand the temperature required for heat treatment.

Put the perry, sugar, vanilla, lemon zest, and honey into a large pan with 1 cup water. Stir, bring to a boil, then simmer for 5 minutes.

Peel the pears and add them immediately to the pan. Cover with a piece of scrunched-up parchment paper to keep them submerged and bring back to a boil. Then reduce the heat and simmer for 25 minutes. Meanwhile, preheat the oven to 325°F (160°C).

Pack the pears tightly into jars and push down to leave space for the syrup to completely cover them. (It will be easier to fit them into bigger jars, or you can cut the pears in half lengthwise.) Fill the jars with the syrup, ensuring that all the pears are fully submerged, then place their lids on top, but do not seal.

Lay a dish cloth or kitchen towel in the bottom of a roasting pan and put the warm sterilized jars on top, spacing them well apart. Add water to the pan to a depth of about ¾in (2cm). Bake in the oven for 30 minutes, then remove and carefully seal the jars with their lids while still hot.

WARM POACHED PEARS WITH MASCARPONE ICE CREAM

This dessert is ideal for a lazy supper—you can make it all in advance, and just reheat the pears before serving.

Serves 6
For the ice cream
4 egg yolks
18oz (500g) mascarpone
²⁄₃ cup heavy cream
1 cup confectioner's (icing) sugar
½ teaspoon ground cinnamon
good grating of nutmeg
6 Vanilla and Perry Poached Pears (see left)

Put all of the ice cream ingredients into a large bowl and, using a hand-held electric whisk, beat for about 1 minute until smooth and creamy. Pour into a plastic lidded container and place into the freezer. Freeze for 1½ to 2 hours, or until partially frozen.

Remove from the freezer and, using the whisk, beat again to break up the ice crystals. Put the ice cream back into the freezer until completely frozen.

Place the pears into a saucepan with some of their syrup. Heat gently until hot. Meanwhile, remove the ice cream from the freezer to soften slightly. Serve the hot pears with a good scoop of the ice cream and a little of the syrup.

Mulled Spiced Pears and Figs

I really enjoy these spiced fruits as an accompaniment to a bowl of good vanilla ice cream; however, what I like best is to open a jar at Christmas time to eat with cold meats and a wedge of Manchego cheese.

Makes about 1 quart (1 liter)
Keeps for at least a year

2/3 cup white wine vinegar

1 1/3 cups ruby Port

1 cup light brown sugar

1 heaping teaspoon mixed spice (try a blend of
   ground coriander, cloves, ginger, and nutmeg)

1 cinnamon stick

7 just-ripe pears, peeled, cored, and cut into 8 wedges

9oz (250g) ready-to-eat dried figs, halved

Put the vinegar, Port, and 2/3 cup water in a pan with the sugar and spices. Stir, bring to a boil, then reduce the heat and simmer for 35 minutes.

Add the pears, bring back to a boil, and cook for 2 to 3 minutes. Transfer the pears to a bowl and stir in the figs.

Boil the liquid in the pan for about 10 to 15 minutes until halved in volume. Pack the fruit tightly into warm sterilized jars, top off with the syrup, and seal.

Moroccan Prune Chutney

I like the combination of fresh plums and dried prunes in this chutney—the plums add a burst of fruitiness and the prunes add richness and intensity. I love using harissa in tagines, but now I also have a ready-made taste of Morocco to spice up cold cuts and cheese or to dollop on the side of quickly grilled lamb or sausages.

Makes about 2 quarts (2 liters)
Keeps for at least a year

2lb (1kg) dark plums, halved, pitted, and chopped

2 large cooking apples, peeled, cored, and chopped

2 onions, peeled and finely chopped

4 garlic cloves, peeled and sliced

1 cup pitted soft dried prunes, halved

1 cup golden raisins

2¾ cups packed dark brown sugar

2 tablespoons harissa, plus extra to taste

1 cinnamon stick

1 heaping teaspoon mixed spice (try a blend of ground coriander, cinnamon, cloves, ginger, and nutmeg)

2 cups malt vinegar

Put all the ingredients in a pan and bring to a boil. Reduce the heat to a simmer and cook for 2 to 2¼ hours, or until thick enough to leave a trail when you run a wooden spoon through it. (There should be some liquid left, however, as the chutney will thicken up in the jars.) You will need to stir the chutney occasionally to prevent it from sticking, but do so with caution, as it does bubble up!

Taste a little, adding extra harissa if you like, then ladle into warm sterilized jars and seal. You can eat it immediately, but it will improve over time.

GLAZED MOROCCAN LAMB STEAKS WITH COUSCOUS

A great, quick-to-prepare supper to serve for a casual meal with friends. If you want to be really speedy, then marinate for just 10 minutes.

Serves 4

2 garlic cloves, chopped

1 teaspoon cumin seeds

2 tablespoons Moroccan Prune Chutney (see left), or another spiced fruity chutney

2½ tablespoons olive oil

splash of red or white wine

salt and freshly ground black pepper

4 boneless lamb steaks

1 red bell pepper, cored and chopped

2 zucchini, chopped

6 green onions, chopped

3 tablespoons pine nuts

1 cup couscous

2 tablespoons butter

4 pinches of ground cinnamon

1 cup hot vegetable stock

In a large dish, mix together the garlic, cumin seeds, chutney, 1½ tablespoons olive oil, the wine, and salt and pepper. Add the steaks and turn to thoroughly coat them with the mixture. Leave to marinate for 30 minutes.

Meanwhile, heat the remaining oil in a frying pan and gently cook the red pepper for 5 minutes. Add the zucchini, scallions, and pine nuts and stir-fry very gently until the zucchini is just tender.

Put the couscous into a bowl with the butter, cinnamon, some salt and pepper, and the freshly made hot stock. Stir, then cover with plastic wrap and leave to swell for 5 minutes.

Heat a non-stick ridged grill pan until very hot, then cook the lamb steaks for 3 minutes on each side. Add the vegetables to the couscous and fluff with a fork to combine. Serve with the lamb steaks.

Roasted Tomato Sauce Two Ways

This recipe for the tomato base can be used to make a rich roasted tomato sauce or a ketchup, or both (see page 117). It's packed with tomatoes and olive oil, and roasting the vegetables really adds a depth and sweetness. It's also, of course, much healthier than any store-bought sauce or ketchup and therefore great for children—I'm pleased to say that mine wolf it down every time! You can use a mix of different tomato varieties, but be sure you include plenty of beefsteaks as well as the small sweeter ones.

5½lb (2.5kg) ripe tomatoes

4 medium red onions, peeled and sliced fairly thickly

2 celery stalks, cut into 1in (2.5cm) lengths

6 whole unpeeled garlic cloves

2in (5cm) piece of fresh ginger, peeled and chopped

1 red chili pepper, seeded and chopped

small handful of fresh thyme leaves

2 tablespoons dark brown sugar

salt and freshly ground black pepper

4 tablespoons olive oil

3 tablespoons red wine vinegar

Preheat the oven to 400°F (200°C). Use a knife to slice a cross on the bottom of each tomato and put into a large bowl. Pour in freshly boiled water to cover and leave for 30 seconds or so for their skins to split. Drain off the water and remove the skins. Cut the larger ones in half.

Place the onions, celery, garlic, ginger, chili pepper, and thyme on two roasting pans to a depth of at least ¾in (2cm). Lay the tomatoes on top, sprinkle with the sugar and some salt and pepper, and drizzle with the oil and vinegar. Cover the pans with foil and bake for 40 minutes.

Remove the pans from the oven, lift the foil, and toss everything together. Cover again, return to the oven, and bake for another 20 to 30 minutes, or until the vegetables are softened.

Remove the pans from the oven and discard the foil. When cool enough to handle, pick out the garlic cloves and squeeze the soft garlic purée out of the skins and onto the tomatoes, then discard the skins.

Transfer everything to a large pan and blend with a hand-held blender until coarsely puréed (or use a food processor). Now you can use the base to make the ketchup or pasta sauce (page 117).

1) Tomato and Basil Pasta Sauce

Makes 1¾ quarts (1.8 liters)
Keeps for up to 6 months

Preheat the oven to 325°F (160°C). Bring one quantity of the roasted tomato base (see page 114) up to boiling point, add a generous handful of chopped fresh basil leaves, and taste for seasoning. Pour into 4 x 16oz (500ml) warm sterilized jars, half close with their lids (a half turn allows for some steam to get out), and place in a roasting pan lined with a dish cloth or kitchen towel, spacing them well apart. Add boiling water to the pan to a depth of about ¾in (2cm) and bake for 25 minutes. Seal and cool before storing in a cool, dark place.

2) Tomato Ketchup

Makes 1¾ quarts (1.8 liters)
Keeps for up to 6 months

Put one quantity of the roasted tomato base (see page 114) into a pan with ½ cup red wine vinegar, ½ cup dark brown sugar, ⅓ teaspoon ground cloves, 1 teaspoon ground coriander, and 1 cup water. Bring to a boil, then simmer for 20 minutes. Purée using a hand-held blender or a traditional blender or food processor. Pour into 4 x 16oz (500ml) warm sterilized bottles and seal.

For a fiery version of this ketchup, add 2 to 3 chili peppers.

Sweet and Sour Pickled Vegetables

A jar of these pickled vegetables makes a great present. The radishes do bleed their color into the vinegar so, if you prefer, leave them out and use a whole cucumber. I recommend baby carrots for this as their small size looks more attractive in the jar, but thickly sliced regular carrots do the job just as well.

Makes about 1¾ quarts (1.8 liters)
Keeps for at least a year

1⅔ cups white wine vinegar

¾ cup cider vinegar

½ cup dark brown sugar

4 bay leaves

10 peppercorns

½ tablespoon coriander seeds

1 heaping tablespoon kosher salt

5oz (150g) shallots, plunged into boiling water then peeled

1 small cauliflower, broken into smallish florets

½lb (250g) baby carrots, trimmed and cut in half lengthwise
    or ½lb regular carrots, cut into thick, diagonal slices

1 fennel bulb, trimmed and sliced

½ cucumber, halved lengthwise, seeded and sliced thickly

6oz (175g) radishes

Pour the vinegars into a large pan with 1 cup water and add the sugar, bay leaves, peppercorns, coriander seeds, and salt. Bring slowly to a boil and when the liquid is boiling rapidly, add the shallots. Cook for 2 minutes, then add the cauliflower and carrots. Stir into the liquid and cook for 1½ minutes, then stir in the fennel and cucumber. Cook for another 1½ minutes, then remove from the heat.

Using a slotted spoon, transfer the vegetables into warm sterilized jars, interspersing them with the raw radishes. Pour in the hot liquid to cover the vegetables completely. Seal the jars and store for 2 weeks before eating.

Piccalilli

I always think of this as grown-ups' relish because it never appealed to me until I hit my 20s, when I suddenly wondered why I hadn't enjoyed it before. This one is fairly mild; increase the quantity of mustard if you want something that packs more of a punch.

Makes 2¾ quarts (2.7 liters)
Keeps for at least a year

14oz (400g) shallots
2 smallish cauliflowers, broken into very small florets
1¼lb (600g) zucchini, cut into ¾in (2cm) cubes
¾lb (350g) green beans, destrung and cut diagonally into ¾in lengths
1 cup sea salt
1½ quarts (1.5 liters) cider vinegar
2 garlic cloves, crushed
1½in (4cm) piece of fresh ginger, peeled and grated
2 tablespoons black mustard seeds
½ teaspoon ground allspice
1 cup superfine sugar
⅓ cup all-purpose flour
1 heaping tablespoon ground turmeric
2 tablespoons English mustard

Pour boiled water over the shallots. Leave for a minute or so, then drain and peel off the skins. Cut each in half and put into a large bowl with the cauliflower, zucchini, and runner beans. In a large pitcher, dissolve the salt in 1⅓ cups boiling water, add 2 quarts (2 liters) cold water, and pour in the vegetables. Leave overnight.

The next day, pour the vinegar into a large pan and add the garlic, ginger, mustard seeds, allspice, and sugar. Bring to a boil. While the vinegar heats, drain the salty water from the vegetables and rinse well. Add them to a boiling vinegar. Cover the pan while the liquid comes back to the boil, then remove the lid and boil the vegetables for 5 minutes, or until the cauliflower is just tender, but still with a little bite. Drain them, reserving the vinegar in a pitcher.

Mix the flour, turmeric, and mustard with 6 to 8 tablespoons water. Add a little of the warm vinegar and pour into a pan. Whisk the mixture over the heat, gradually incorporating the remaining vinegar. Bring to a boil, then simmer for about 5 minutes. Pour the mixture over the vegetables and stir.

Divide the vegetables and delicious sauce between warm sterilized jars and seal. Store for 6 weeks before using.

PRESERVED HAM SERVED WITH PICCALILLI AND TOAST

This combination should be positioned next to bacon and eggs or steak and potatoes on the culinary-matches-made-in-heaven list! It's great as an appetizer, or even better—as we ate it recently with friends—with a few cheeses, for an informal weekend lunch. It's also a good way to use up any leftovers from a roast ham, and it freezes beautifully. Don't be tempted to buy inexpensive ham, as you can really taste the difference.

Serves 6

4½ sticks (500g) butter
1lb (500g) piece of cooked and cold ham, coarsely chopped
½ cup parsley, leaves removed and chopped
good grating of nutmeg
salt and freshly ground black pepper
2 teaspoons wholegrain mustard

To serve

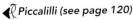 *Piccalilli (see page 120)*
6 thick slices of sourdough or country-style bread, toasted

Melt the butter gently in a pan. Line a sieve with a piece of cheesecloth and pour the butter in, allowing the clarified butter to drip into a bowl below.

Meanwhile, put the ham, parsley, nutmeg, and a good grinding of pepper in a food processor. Add half the clarified butter and process until the mixture is combined but remains coarsely textured. Then taste, adding extra seasoning if needed.

Using a spoon, pack the mixture into 6 x ½ cup ramekins (or one larger dish, if you prefer) and smooth over the top. Mix the remaining clarified butter with the mustard and pour in the top to cover the ham mixture completely. Chill until cold, then serve with Piccalilli and toast, or freeze for later use.

Fruity Pickled Red Cabbage

I've moved away from tradition here and gone for a fruity pickled cabbage with a kick—a great accompaniment to leftover roast pork or beef. Just pop a buttery baked potato on the side and you've got Monday's dinner all set.

Makes 2 quarts (2 liters)
Keeps for a year

2¾lb (1.2kg) red cabbage, quartered, cored, and thinly sliced
2 heaping tablespoons salt
1 quart (1 liter) red wine vinegar
5 tablespoons dark brown sugar
2 pinches of crushed red pepper flakes
good pinch of ground cloves
zest and juice of ½ orange
1 cinnamon stick

Shred the cabbage finely, then put into a bowl, sprinkling the salt between layers. Weigh down the cabbage with a plate topped with a couple of cans and leave overnight to release any water.

Meanwhile, heat all the remaining ingredients in a pan until the sugar has dissolved. Set aside to cool and infuse.

The next day, rinse the cabbage thoroughly to remove the salt and pat dry with paper towels. Pack the cabbage tightly into warm sterilized jars and pour in the pickling liquid. Seal and store for a month before using.

White Balsamic Pickled Peppers

I always keep a jar of pepper antipasto in my kitchen cabinet to liven up a lunch or impromptu appetizer. However, I am increasingly alarmed at how expensive the Italian deli-style jars are. A few experiments led me to this version—just add a dash of extra virgin olive oil and some basil and you've got an instant bruschetta topping. By all means use normal balsamic vinegar—it adds color but does the same job as the white version.

Makes about 1 quart (1 liter)
Keeps for 4 months

8 red or yellow bell peppers or a mix
½ cup white balsamic vinegar
⅓ cup white wine vinegar
1½ tablespoons granulated sugar
½ teaspoon sea salt and freshly ground black pepper

Preheat the oven to 425°F (220°C). Place the whole peppers into a roasting pan and bake for 40 minutes, or until the skins of the peppers are blistered, turning them over half way through the cooking time. Put the hot peppers into a bowl and cover with plastic wrap.

Meanwhile, put the vinegars, sugar, and salt into a small pan, bring to a boil, and simmer for 5 minutes.

Remove the peppers from the bowl one at a time and peel off their skins, working over the bowl to catch the precious juices. Remove the seeds and cut each pepper into about 4 wedges. Pack into warm sterilized jars.

Strain the pepper juices from the bowl into the vinegar pan, along with a good grind of pepper, and stir in. Pour the vinegar over the peppers so that they are totally submerged (you can always pour a little extra vinegar in, if you don't have quite enough). Seal and store.

Brambly Hedge Jelly

My favorite childhood books were those from the Brambly Hedge series by Jill Barklem—the most magical stories, beautifully illustrated, of field mice living in the hedges. I can imagine this jelly being made by Daisy Woodmouse and eaten in the stump of a tree with some rosehip tea—and it's an ideal Sunday afternoon accompaniment to toast. I make an exception to the rules of jelly making with this one and squeeze the bag to release more of the blackberry juices—as it's very dark crimson in color, you can get away with it being a bit cloudy.

Makes 1½ quarts (1.5 liters)
Keeps for up to a year

2lb (1kg) cooking apples, unpeeled and uncored, coarsely chopped
2lb (1kg) plump blackberries
about 5 cups granulated sugar

Put the apples and blackberries into a large pan with 1 quart (1 liter) water and bring to a boil. Reduce the heat and simmer for 25 minutes, or until the fruit is soft and pulpy. Pour carefully into a jelly bag and leave for at least 6 hours. Toward the end of this time, give the bag a good squeeze to release some more of the blackberry juice.

Measure the liquid in a large pitcher and pour back into a large saucepan. Heat until just coming to a boil, then add 2¼ cups sugar for every 2 cups juice yielded. Stir over low heat to dissolve, then increase the heat until the liquid forms a rolling boil. Boil for about 15 to 20 minutes, or until the jelly reaches setting point. Skim off any surface residue, pour into warm sterilized jars, and seal.

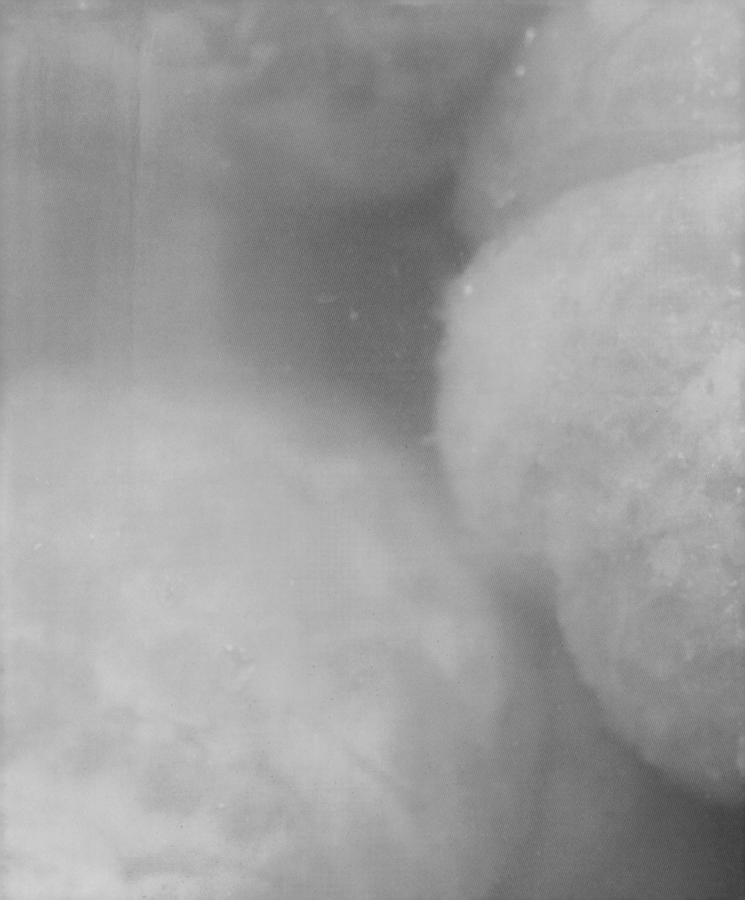

Winter

Easy Seville Marmalade

This method is perfect for those who, like me, want a quick-to-prepare breakfast marmalade that will suit everyone's taste, even that of the fussiest marmalade connoisseur. The fact that you can chop everything in the food processor and that you don't need to deal with sticky seeds in cheesecloth will be, I hope, a revelation! If, however, you are a fan of thick-shred marmalade, you might want to cut the peel by hand.

Makes about 3 quarts (3 liters)
Keeps for 2 years

2lb (1kg) Seville oranges
3½ cups packed dark brown sugar
5 cups granulated sugar
juice of 1 large lemon

Wash the oranges thoroughly, then remove the knobby bits from the ends and cut each in half. Thoroughly juice the oranges (I use an electric juicer). Discard the seeds and pour the juice into a large bowl. Cut the juiced halved oranges in half again and remove any remaining seeds. Put the quarters into a food processor and process until finely chopped (you might need to do this in two batches), or cut the peel into shreds by hand. Add the chopped flesh, peel, and pith to the juice in the bowl and pour in 2½ quarts (2.5 liters) of cold water. Stir, cover, and leave to macerate overnight.

The next day, transfer everything into a large pan and bring to a boil (this will take about 15 minutes). Once at boiling point, reduce the heat and simmer for another 1½ hours, or until the peel is soft.

Add the sugars and lemon juice and stir over the heat until the sugar has dissolved. Increase the heat to bring the liquid to a rolling boil. Do not stir the marmalade from this point on. After 20 minutes, test to see if it has reached setting point. If it hasn't, leave for another few minutes, then test again.

Remove the pan from the heat, leave to stand for 10 minutes, then ladle the marmalade, or pour it from a pitcher, into sterilized jars and seal.

Variation: Orange Blossom Marmalade

Omit the dark brown sugar and increase the quantity of granulated sugar to 9 cups. Follow the method for Easy Seville Marmalade (see left), but stir 3 tablespoons orange flower water into the bowl with the oranges before leaving overnight. Continue as per the recipe.

Variation: Three Fruit Marmalade

The clementines make this mix more mellow than traditional orange marmalade and, also, ideal to use for the Warm Marmalade Upside-down Cake on page 136.

Follow the recipe for Easy Seville Marmalade (see left), but use only 1lb (500g) Seville oranges and add about 6 clementines and 2 large lemons. Omit the dark brown sugar and increase the quantity of granulated sugar to 9 cups.

I chop the peel by hand for this one as I like to see the different colors more clearly, but you can use a food processor if you are short on time.

Stop-gap Marmalade

I know most marmalade makers insist that Sevilles are the only oranges to use, but it's handy to have a year-round, no-frills recipe to turn to when supplies of marmalade are running low. This is not quite as full flavored as the real thing, but it's a lot nicer than supermarket versions and takes a matter of minutes to prepare. Peel that has been cut up into shreds by hand looks prettier but, if you want to cheat, then use a fine slicer on a food processor.

Makes about 1½ quarts (1.5 liters)
Keeps for 2 years
1½lb (700g) oranges
2 large lemons
2¼ cups dark brown sugar
1 cup granulated sugar

Wash the oranges and lemons thoroughly, then remove the knobby bits from the ends and cut in half. Juice the fruit, discard the seeds, and pour the juice into a large pan. Cut the juiced halves in half again and remove any remaining seeds. Put the quarters through the fine slicer attachment of a food processor or cut by hand into fine or thicker shreds, as you prefer. Add to the juice in the pan and pour in 1¼ quarts (1.25 liters) cold water. Bring to a boil, then reduce the heat and simmer the juices and peel gently for 1¼ hours, or until the peel is completely soft.

Add the sugars and stir until dissolved. Then, increase the heat to bring the liquid to a rolling boil. Do not stir the marmalade from this point on. After the marmalade has been boiling for 8 to 10 minutes, test to see if it has reached setting point. If it hasn't, leave for another few minutes and test again.

Remove the pan from the heat, leave to stand for 10 minutes, then ladle the marmalade, or pour it from a pitcher, into sterilized jars and seal.

Preserved Lemons

If you are a fan of Moroccan food then this will be a great addition to your pantry. Preserved lemons add authenticity to all sorts of North African tagines as well as Middle Eastern salads.

Makes about 1 quart (1 liter)
Keeps for 2 years
8 large organic lemons, scrubbed well
⅔ cup sea salt
2 teaspoons pink peppercorns in brine, drained
6 fresh bay leaves

Quarter four of the lemons lengthwise and juice the remaining four. Pack the lemon quarters into warm sterilized jars, sprinkling the salt, peppercorns, and bay leaves between the layers. Add the lemon juice then top off with water so that the lemons are submerged. Seal and store for 3 months before using.

WARM MARMALADE UPSIDE-DOWN CAKE

This is particularly tasty when served with a dollop of crème fraîche. Use any kind of marmalade you like for this recipe, except perhaps a dark one, as it would conceal the pretty oranges arranged on the top. I haven't tried making this cake with other fruits, but see no reason why you couldn't use halved apricots or plums (and the equivalent jam) in the summer or autumn months.

Serves 8 to 10
For the base
3 tablespoons butter
¼ cup superfine sugar
2 heaping tablespoons Easy Seville or Three Fruit Marmalade (see page 133)
2 to 3 large sweet oranges
For the cake
1¾ sticks (40g) very soft butter
4 large eggs, at room temperature
3 heaping tablespoons Easy Seville or Three Fruit Marmalade (see page 133)
2 tablespoons milk
¾ cup superfine sugar
½ cup ground almonds
1⅔ cups self-rising flour
1 heaping teaspoon baking powder

Preheat the oven to 350°F (180°C). Grease a 9 x 2½in (23 x 6cm) deep round cake pan with a removable bottom.

In a pan, melt the butter, sugar, and marmalade for the base, then pour the mixture into the pan and spread it out. Peel the oranges, remove the pith, and, using a serrated knife, slice them very thinly. Remove the seeds. Arrange the orange slices in the pan, overlapping them to cover the whole of the base.

Put all the cake ingredients into the bowl of an electric mixer, sifting in the flour and baking powder last. Turn the speed setting to low, just to incorporate the flour, then increase it to medium and beat the mixture for about 2 minutes, or until fluffy. Spoon the mixture carefully into the pan and spread it out, making a slight dip in the center. Place the pan onto a baking sheet (to prevent spillage), and bake for 35 minutes.

Open the oven door and, as quickly as you can, cover the top of the cake with a piece of foil (this will keep it from burning). Bake for another 25 minutes, or until a skewer inserted into the center of the cake comes out completely clean.

Leave the cake to cool for about 10 minutes, then slide a knife around the edge, place a plate on the top, turn upside down, and release the springs. The cake should come away easily. Serve warm with half-and-half or crème fraîche.

BRÛLÉED MARMALADE TART

This is a lovely lemony tart that has just a hint of orange and pretty flecks of peel throughout. It's best to use a kitchen blowtorch for the brûlée top, unless you have a really good broiler. Feel free to omit the brûléed top if you like; it's just as delicious without. You can make the pastry case up to 24 hours ahead if you wish.

Serves 6
13oz (375g) ready-made tart shell
4 heaping tablespoons Three Fruit Marmalade (see page 133),
    or other orange marmalade (but not dark)
¼ cup + 3 tablespoons heavy cream
½ cup superfine sugar, plus 3 to 4 tablespoons for sprinkling
5 eggs
juice of 5 large lemons

Make sure the shell is fridge cold. Roll out to ¼in (5mm) thickness and line a 9 x 2½in (23 x 6cm) deep tart pan, making sure the pastry sits slightly higher than the edge of the pan to allow for shrinkage. (You can do this by pinching the edges between your fingers.) Chill for 30 minutes. Meanwhile, preheat the oven to 400°F (200°C).

Remove the pastry case from the fridge, line with parchment paper, fill with baking beans, and bake for 10 minutes. Remove the beans and paper and cook for another 5 to 10 minutes, or until pale golden. Remove from the oven and cool.

If you have made the pastry case earlier, preheat the oven to 325°F (160°C). Gently melt the marmalade in a pan, then stir in the cream and sugar and warm gently. Meanwhile, beat the eggs and lemon juice in a bowl, then strain through a sieve into a large pitcher. Add the cream mixture, stirring to combine.

Put the pastry case, still in its pan, onto a baking sheet, and pour in the egg-and-cream mixture until it reaches the top. (You might have a little left over, but be sure that you use up all the lovely marmeladey bits that may have accumulated in the bottom of the pitcher.) Bake in the oven for 25 to 35 minutes, or until just set. (The center of the tart should wobble slightly when you jiggle the pan.) Remove the tart from the oven and cool, but do not chill.

Transfer the tart to a plate about 15 minutes before you are ready to serve it. Sprinkle with the extra sugar and use a blow torch to caramelize the top. If you want to brûlée the tart under the broiler, make sure that it is very hot, and put a collar of foil around the edge of the pastry to prevent it from burning. Leave to cool again for 10 minutes, then serve with half-and-half.

Dried Orange Peel

I first tasted dried orange peel when a good friend, cookbook author Alex Mackay, sent me some to try. This method of drying the peel is based on Alex's, from his book *Cooking in Provence*. It peps up anything from a tomato sauce to a chocolate dessert—I particularly love it added to casseroles and stews.

Makes enough to fill a ½ quart (500ml) jar
Keeps for at least a year
5 to 6 large oranges

Preheat the oven to 225°F (110°C).

Remove the zest, but not the pith, of the oranges in long strips using a vegetable peeler. Scatter the zest strips in a single layer on either a non-stick baking sheet or a cake rack over a baking sheet. Place into the oven and leave for 3 to 4 hours, or until the pieces of peel are dry enough to snap in your fingers.

Allow to cool, then store in a sealed jar or an airtight container. The dried orange peel will keep virtually forever as long as the container is airtight.

BEEF WITH ORANGE AND PRUNES

There are a few foods that really hit the jackpot when you need to be taken to a warm and happy place on a Friday evening after a long week, and this, without a doubt, is at the top on my list. All you need now is a large glass of Spanish red and your PJs! If you like, you can make a big batch and freeze it in smaller portions, then just defrost and reheat as needed. Canned beef consommé is a great time-saving alternative to making your own stock—and it's much tastier than bouillon cubes. Keep a couple of cans in your cupboard at all times.

Serves 6 to 8

2 tablespoons all-purpose flour
salt and freshly ground black pepper
2¾lb (1.25kg) stewing steak, cut into 2½ to 3in (6–8cm) chunks
¼ cup shortening
2 medium onions, peeled and sliced
3 large carrots, peeled and cut into large chunks
2 celery stalks, trimmed and cut into chunks
2 garlic cloves, peeled and chopped
1¾ cups Guinness
2 sprigs of thyme
2 bay leaves
3 strips of Dried Orange Peel (see opposite), or zest of 1 orange
1 x 14oz (398ml) can of pitted prunes in syrup
1 x 14oz (398ml) can of beef consommé
1 teaspoon redcurrant jelly

Preheat the oven to 325°F (160°C). Put the flour into a large bowl and mix with plenty of salt and pepper. Add the steak and toss together using your hands.

Heat a walnut-sized piece of the shortening in a heavy-bottomed frying pan until smoking hot. Cook the stewing steak in batches until caramelized and rich brown in color on all sides. Remove the browned beef chunks to a large ovenproof casserole. Add a little more shortening as required.

Add the onions, carrots, celery, and garlic to the frying pan and stir-fry them over medium heat for 5 to 7 minutes. Put them into a bowl and set aside.

Pour the Guinness into the frying pan and bring to a boil, scraping up any beefy leftovers in the bottom of the pan. Pour into the casserole, then add the herbs, dried orange peel, drained prunes and a third of their juice, the consommé, and the redcurrant jelly. Heat on the stove to simmering point.

Cover and cook in the oven for 1 hour. Remove the casserole from the oven and stir in the vegetables, then cook for another hour, or until the beef is tender. Season to taste (and add a little more prune juice at this stage if you like), then serve with baked potatoes and green vegetables.

Pooh's Lemonade

My mother-in-law, affectionately called "Pooh," makes the best lemon cordial. She made it in great vats for our wedding as a refreshing alternative to the usual sickly-sweet orange juice usually that is sometimes offered. If you don't want the bother of sterilizing bottles, you can store it in plastic containers in the freezer—just defrost as needed and keep it in the fridge.

Makes about 1¾ quarts (1.7 liters)
Keeps for 3 weeks in the fridge,
or can be frozen

6 lemons
3½ cups granulated sugar
2 level teaspoons citric acid

Peel three of the lemons using a potato peeler, reserving the peel. Under the palm of your hand, roll all six lemons on a cutting board to slacken a little (so they will yield more juice). Halve the lemons and squeeze out the juice into a bowl.

Put the sugar into a large pither, add 1¼ quarts (1.25 liters) boiling water, and stir to dissolve, then stir in the citric acid and lemon juice.

Divide the peel strips between warm sterilized bottles (or plastic containers if freezing). Pour the liquid into the bottles using a funnel (only three-quarters full if freezing) and seal.

Store either in a cool place or in the freezer. When ready to drink, dilute to taste with sparkling or still water—or use to make pink lemonade (see right).

PINK LEMONADE

Obviously this is a perfect drink for the summer, but it's in this chapter because it uses citrus fruits that are in season in winter. It's as pretty as a picture when topped with pomegranate seeds and is ideal to serve as an almost non-alcoholic cocktail for Christmas drinks. Grenadine gives a great flavor, but you could substitute a dash of pomegranate or raspberry juice if you prefer.

Makes 4 glasses
 *¾ cup Pooh's Lemonade (see left)*
3 teaspoons grenadine
2¾ cups sparkling water
Pomegranate seeds or raspberries, to garnish (optional)

Pour the lemonade and grenadine into a large pitcher and add some ice. Add the sparkling water and taste for strength, adding more water if necessary.

To serve, pour into four glasses and add a couple of raspberries or a few pomegranate seeds to each glass, if you wish.

Limeade

As it's quick to make, this limeade—a variation of the lemonade recipe on page 145—can be whipped up in time for an impromptu get-together. It's also great in cocktails—mixed with a shot of gin and lots of mint and soda water, for example. Store in sterilized bottles or in plastic containers in the freezer—simply defrost as required and keep in the fridge.

Makes about 2 quarts (2 liters)
Keeps for 3 weeks in the fridge, or can be frozen
6 limes
3 lemons
3 cups granulated sugar
2 level teaspoons citric acid

Peel 4 of the limes using a potato peeler, reserving the peel. Under the palm of your hand, roll all of the fruit on a cutting board to slacken a little (so they will yield more juice). Cut the fruits in half and squeeze out the juice into a bowl.

Put the sugar into a large pitcher, add 1¼ quarts (1.25 liters) of boiling water, and stir to dissolve, then stir in the citric acid and lemon and lime juice.

Divide the peel strips between warm sterilized bottles (or plastic containers if freezing). Pour the liquid into the bottles using a funnel (only three-quarters full if freezing) and seal.

Store either in a cool place or in the freezer. When ready to drink, dilute to taste with still or sparkling water.

Clementines in Brandy

A great present for relatives that are tricky to buy for, this is also a great preserve to keep in the kitchen cabinet for a last-minute dessert. Served simply with ice cream, it makes a refreshing end to a heavy meal and requires no effort from the cook!

Makes 1½ quarts (1.5 liters)
Keeps for 2 years
1⅓ cups dark brown sugar
2 cups brandy
12 to 14 clementines

Put the sugar into a pan with ¾ cup water and dissolve over low heat, stirring occasionally. Remove the pan from the heat and add the brandy.

Meanwhile, peel the clementines, removing as much of the pith as you can. Pack tightly into warm sterilized jars, then pour in the brandy syrup. If there is not enough to completely cover the fruit, top off with a little more brandy or water. Seal the jars.

Sweet Thai Chili Paste

I have to pay tribute to Peter Gordon of the Sugar Club in London for providing the inspiration for this recipe. I have made his sweet chili sauce a few times and it is magnificent. However, living in the country, I find it difficult to get ahold of some of his ingredients, so I've come up with my own version, using ingredients that are easy to come by locally. I have also reduced the sugar levels from traditional sweet chili sauce. This paste can be used as a marinade, a curry base, or as a dipping sauce. We love it smeared over drumsticks and baked in the oven for an hour or so, or as a stir-fry paste for beef. You can also use it to make the curry on page 150. If you want it feistier, remove only half the chili seeds.

Makes about 1 quart (1 liter)
Keeps for up to a year

2 garlic bulbs, separated into cloves and peeled
12 long red chili peppers, halved lengthwise and seeded
3 x 3in (3 x 8cm) pieces of fresh ginger, peeled and cut into ¾in (2cm) pieces
1 x large bunch of fresh cilantro, stems and leaves chopped
4 lemongrass stems, trimmed and finely chopped
9 lime leaves (fresh if possible, otherwise freeze-dried,
    but not really finely shredded)
1¾ cups packed dark brown sugar
6 tablespoons rice wine vinegar
4 tablespoons soy sauce
4 tablespoons fish sauce
juice of 2 limes

Put the garlic, chili peppers, ginger, cilantro, lemongrass, and lime leaves into a food processor and process, scraping down the sides of the bowl, until you have a fine paste.

Put the sugar and ¾ cup water into a large, deep frying pan and heat gently until the sugar has dissolved, then increase the heat and boil for about 5 minutes, or until the syrup has the consistency of honey.

Carefully add the paste to the pan (it might spit a little) and stir-fry for another 5 to 7 minutes, or until the liquid has evaporated.

Add the rice wine vinegar, soy sauce, fish sauce, lime juice, and 1⅔ cups water and boil, stirring, for another 15 to 20 minutes, or until you have a thick but pourable paste. Spoon into warm sterilized jars and seal.

SHRIMP, EGGPLANT, AND PEPPER CURRY

A great shrimp curry that is thrown together in minutes is the best Friday night supper. This one can be made with cooked shrimp if you prefer, but will need slightly less cooking time.

Serves 4

1½ tablespoons peanut oil
1 onion, peeled and sliced
1 medium eggplant, cut into 1½in (4cm) cubes
   or 6 baby eggplants, cut into wedges
1 green bell pepper, cored, seeded and cut into chunks
2 tablespoons Sweet Thai Chili Paste (see page 149)
   or a store-bought Thai paste
1 x 14oz (398ml) can of coconut milk
2 handfuls of cherry tomatoes
24 raw peeled jumbo shrimp
1½ tablespoons fish sauce
squeeze of lime juice
handful of fresh cilantro or torn basil leaves, to serve

Heat the oil in a saucepan, then soften the onion for 3 minutes before adding the eggplant and pepper. Continue to stir-fry gently for about 5 minutes.

Add the chili paste and stir-fry for another 1 to 2 minutes, then stir in the creamy top of the coconut milk. Simmer for about 10 minutes.

Stir in the remainder of the coconut milk, bring back to simmering point, then add the tomatoes and cook for 3 minutes.

Add the shrimp and cook them in the sauce until they have turned pink and are piping hot. Just before serving, stir in the fish sauce and lime. Serve the curry sprinkled with the herbs.

Lemon Curd

My mother-in-law is a fantastic cook, and always produces incredible meals for us all with ease. One of her secrets is that she uses clever shortcuts, tried and tested over the years. She swears that you can make lemon curd in the microwave, beating the mixture every minute or two until thick. However, as I'm awful at remembering to check, I always end up with either scrambled egg or a boiled-over mess to clean up. Use a microwave if you dare—it will certainly save you time—but if, like me, you're a scaredy-cat, try the method below instead!

Makes about 1 quart (1 liter)
Unopened, keeps for up to 4 weeks in the fridge
2¼ sticks (250g) butter
juice and zest of 5 to 6 organic lemons (you need ¾ cup juice)
5 large eggs
1¼ cups superfine sugar

Put the butter into a large heatproof bowl over a pan of barely simmering water and melt. Meanwhile, put the juice, zest, eggs, and sugar into a bowl and, using a whisk, beat together thoroughly.

Strain this mixture through a sieve into the butter and whisk over the heat for 30 to 35 minutes, or until thick enough to just coat the back of a spoon (it should have the consistency of a runny white sauce).

Pour, while warm, into warm sterilized jars, then seal and store in the fridge for up to a month. Once opened, use within a week.

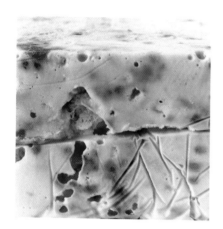

ICED LEMON AND RASPBERRY LOAF

This frozen dessert began as a lemon and blueberry loaf, but one member of our family, who shall remain nameless, is a tad fussy and said he'd prefer it made with raspberries. I have to say that I think he's right, but if you are a blueberry fanatic, you'll be pleased to hear it works with both!

Serves 8

1¼ cups raspberries
1 cup heavy cream
1⅔ cups fresh thick custard
zest and juice of 1 lemon
1¹/3 cups Lemon Curd (see page 153)
6 meringue shells, crushed

Put the raspberries into a small pan, add a dash of water, and heat gently until they have just begun to collapse. Cool.

Combine the cream, custard, lemon zest and juice, and lemon curd in a bowl, then freeze for 1½ hours, or until partially frozen.

Transfer the mixture to a food processor and process, then pour back into the bowl and fold in the raspberries and crushed meringue. Pour into a loaf pan lined with plastic wrap and freeze.

Remove the frozen loaf from the freezer 10 minutes before serving. Turn onto a plate and cut into slices.

Pink Grapefruit, Raspberry, and Blood Orange Curd

I love this combination of fruits, and this vibrant-colored curd looks beautiful spooned into sweet tart cases and topped with raspberries (see opposite) or sliced blood oranges. If you want to make this out of the blood orange season, substitute one extra small grapefruit and omit the orange juice.

Makes about 1¼ quarts (1.25 liters)
Unopened, keeps for up to 4 weeks in the fridge

2½ sticks (275g) butter
1¾ cups raspberries
juice of 2 blood (ruby) oranges
zest and juice of 3 small organic lemons
juice of 1 small pink grapefruit
1⅓ cups superfine sugar
6 large eggs

Put the butter into a large heatproof bowl over a pan of barely simmering water and melt.

Meanwhile, put the raspberries into a bowl and mash with a fork, then add the citrus juices, lemon zest, sugar, and eggs and, using a whisk, beat together until combined.

Strain this mixture through a sieve into the butter and whisk over the heat for about 30 minutes, or until thick enough to just coat the back of a spoon (it should have the consistency of a runny white sauce).

Pour, while hot, into warm sterilized jars, then seal, cool and store in the fridge for up to a month. Once opened, use within a week.

RASPBERRY AND BLOOD ORANGE TARTS

Grand though they look, these are, in fact, the easiest desserts to put together, and make a wonderful last-minute dessert. Keep a stash of the tart cases in the kitchen cabinet, a jar of curd in the fridge, and a pint of raspberries in the freezer and you'll always have a standby to turn to if you haven't got the energy to go to the supermarket!

Makes 8 tarts

8 x 4–5in (10–12cm) ready-baked sweet tart shells
8 heaping tablespoons Pink Grapefruit, Raspberry, and Blood Orange Curd (see left), or other fruit curd of your choice
about 3¼ cups raspberries and/or 2 to 3 peeled and segmented blood oranges

Put the tart shells onto a large plate or individual dessert plates and spoon 1 to 2 tablespoons curd into each.

Top each tart with a raspberry or blood orange segment (or both) and serve immediately, with cold half-and-half if you wish.

Cranberry and Cointreau Relish

One of the prettiest chutneys, with its pink hue, this is perfect for presents at Christmas time or to serve with holiday leftovers. It is also really quick to make compared to most chutneys and relishes.

Makes about 1¼ quarts (1.25 liters)
Keeps for at least a year

splash of olive oil

2 tablespoons butter

1 onion, peeled and chopped

1 large cooking apple, peeled, cored, and chopped

5 cups fresh or frozen cranberries

¾ cup dried cranberries

1⅓ cups granulated sugar

½ teaspoon ground allspice

½ teaspoon ground ginger

1 cinnamon stick

3 tablespoons Cointreau

Heat the oil and butter in a large pan, then add the onion and soften gently for 5 to 8 minutes.

Add all remaining ingredients to the pan with ⅓ cup water, stir, and bring slowly to a boil. Reduce the heat, then simmer for 25 to 30 minutes, or until the apples and cranberries are soft and the relish has thickened slightly. Ladle into warm sterilized jars and seal.

CAMEMBERT, CRANBERRY, AND POPPY SEED BITES

What my mother would call a substantial snack, these bites are great for offering around with drinks, adding to a buffet, or serving as an appetizer with some salad greens. They freeze beautifully: simply make and freeze unbaked. When you're ready to cook them, brush the frozen pockets with melted butter, sprinkle with poppy seeds, and allow an extra few minutes cooking time.

Makes 28

28 filo pastry sheets (each measuring about 10 x 7in/22 x 18cm)

butter, melted, for brushing

9oz (250g) Camembert

5 tablespoons Cranberry and Cointreau Relish (see left)

poppy seeds for sprinkling

Preheat the oven to 400°F (200°C). Lay one filo pastry sheet out on the work surface (keep the others covered with a damp cloth to prevent them from drying out). Brush some melted butter over the sheet and cover with a second sheet. Brush again, then cut in half lengthwise so that you have two long rectangles.

Cut the Camembert into 28 pieces (slice the whole cheese into 14 x ½in (14 x 1cm) slices, discarding the rindy ends, then cut each slice through the middle).

Lay a strip of pastry out with the short end facing you and place a rectangle of cheese at the bottom right of the strip. Top with ½ teaspoon relish, then fold the pastry and cheese over to make a triangular pocket. Keep folding diagonally up the pastry to build up the layers, maintaining the triangle shape. Repeat with the remaining pastry strips and pieces of cheese.

Brush both sides of each filo triangle with butter and sprinkle the tops with poppy seeds. Bake on a baking sheet for 10 to 15 minutes, or until golden brown and crisp.

Cranberry Jelly

I think this is a lovely alternative to cranberry sauce, and it looks beautiful in a glass bowl on the table.

Makes about 1¼ quarts (1.25 liters)
Keeps for up to a year
1lb (500g) cranberries
juice of 1 orange
2½ to 4 cups granulated sugar

Put the cranberries into a pan with the orange juice and 1 quart (1 liter) water and bring slowly to a boil. Reduce the heat and simmer for 20 minutes, or until the cranberries are really soft.

Remove the pan from the heat and, using a potato masher, mash the cranberries in the pan, then transfer to a pitcher and pour slowly into a jelly bag set over a bowl. Leave to strain through overnight.

Measure the liquid in a pitcher, then pour into a pan and bring to a boil. Meanwhile, weigh out the sugar, allowing 2¼ cups sugar per 2 cups juice (for 3 cups juice you would need 3⅓ cups sugar, for example). Add the sugar to the liquid, reduce the heat, and stir until dissolved. Then increase the heat and boil rapidly for about 12 to 18 minutes, or until the jelly has reached setting point.

Ladle the jelly, or pour from a pitcher, into warm sterilized jars and seal.

CRISPY-SKINNED DUCK BREASTS WITH PORT AND CRANBERRY SAUCE

An easy dinner-party dish that requires little effort and receives plenty of appreciation!

4 duck breasts, scored with a sharp knife
1½ tablespoons granulated sugar
1 tablespoon sea salt
1 teaspoon five-spice powder, plus 4 large pinches
4 tablespoons Cranberry Jelly (see left)
zest and juice of 1 orange
⅓ cup Port
1 onion, peeled and thinly sliced
2in (5cm) piece of ginger, peeled and grated
⅔ cup chicken stock
salt and freshly ground black pepper

Put the duck breasts into a non-metallic dish. Mix together the sugar, salt, and 1 teaspoon five-spice powder and rub all over the duck. Cover and refrigerate for 3 to 4 hours.

When you are ready to cook the duck breasts, preheat the oven to 400°F (200°C), and place a baking sheet in the oven to heat up. Meanwhile, put the cranberry jelly, orange juice and zest, and Port into a small pan and simmer for 10 to 15 minutes, or until halved in volume.

Wash the duck breasts thoroughly, then dry them with paper towels and sprinkle with the remaining five-spice powder. Heat a frying pan, add the duck breasts, skin-side down, and cook over low heat for 10 minutes. Then transfer them to the baking sheet, skin-side up this time, and roast for 6 to 8 minutes. Remove from the oven and leave to rest in a warm place (such as a warm plate wrapped loosely with foil) for 10 minutes.

Meanwhile, pour off most of the fat from the duck pan and gently cook the onion and ginger in the remainder until softened. Add the reduced fruity sauce and the stock and simmer for 6 to 8 minutes. Taste and season with salt and pepper as required.

Slice the duck and serve with the sauce, accompanied with some mashed potatoes and green vegetables.

Nutty Granola with Manuka Honey

This granola recipe is great for using up leftover nuts and dried fruits, so it really doesn't matter if you vary the recipe to suit what you've got in the cupboard. Golden raisins, dried cranberries, and dried blueberries are also delicious, but it's best to add all dried fruits after cooking. Manuka is the superfood of the honey world, with an impressive list of healthy benefits, but it's expensive and also has a strong flavor, so feel free to replace all or half of the quantity with regular honey if you wish.

Makes 15 to 20 portions
Keeps for 3 months in a cool place

14oz (400g) jumbo rolled oats
3oz (75g) desiccated coconut
3oz (75g) seeds (I use a mix of sunflower and pumpkin, with a sprinkling of sesame)
7oz (200g) nuts (pecans, almonds, hazelnuts, Brazils, cashews—anything you have)
2/3 cup manuka honey (or a mix of 1/3 cup manuka and 1/3 cup regular honey)
1 stick (110g) butter, melted
4oz (125g) ready-to-eat dried figs, halved
4oz (125g) ready-to-eat dried apricots, halved

Preheat the oven to 300°F (150°C). In a bowl, combine all the ingredients apart from the dried fruits and mix well. Transfer into a roasting pan and toast for about 30 minutes, checking and stirring the granola every 10 minutes. (Be sure that you scrape around the edges of the pan, where the mixture tends to go brown fastest.)

Once the granola is crisp (but it shouldn't smell or taste overly toasted), remove from the oven and leave to cool in the pan, stirring occasionally. Stir in the dried fruits and put into an airtight container.

FRUITY BRUNCH POTS

Make the compote from any fruit you like—poached fruits, raspberries, or apricots, or a mix would also be delicious. It keeps, so it's easiest to prepare the fruit a day ahead and refrigerate it ready for breakfast or brunch in the morning. You don't have to sweeten the yogurt if you prefer it to have a healthy tang, but most people enjoy it best with the added honey.

Makes 2

1½ cups blueberries
6 tablespoons Greek-style yogurt
1 to 2 tablespoons manuka or regular honey
3 tablespoons Nutty Granola with Manuka Honey (see left)

Put ¾ of the pack of blueberries into a pan with a dash of water and simmer until the fruits have burst their skins and the juice looks syrupy. Add the remaining fruit and leave to cool. Just before serving, layer the fruit, yogurt, honey, and granola in 2 glasses.

Boozy Mincemeat

Mincemeat pies grace most tables in England at Christmas time and making your own filling is a sure way to get you feeling festive. I've tried to keep this recipe as basic as possible, as no one wants to spend ages grating and chopping, but I do think that the effort involved in making your own mincemeat pays off.

Keeps for a year

9oz (250g) dried mixed fruit

⅔ cup raisins

⅔ cup golden raisins

1 medium Macintosh apple, cored but
     unpeeled and finely chopped

1 cup light brown sugar

⅔ cup shortening

zest and juice of 1 orange

zest and juice of 1 lemon

¼ teaspoon ground cinnamon

½ teaspoon ground allspice

good grating of nutmeg (about ¼ of a whole one)

3 tablespoons brandy

Put all the ingredients into a large bowl and mix thoroughly. Pack into just warm, but not hot, sterilized jam jars and seal.

Variation: Pear, Cranberry, and Pecan Mincemeat with Rum

Use 2 firm pears in place of the apple, and rum in place of the brandy. Use a half-and-half mix of pecans and almonds and ⅔ cup dried cranberries in addition to all the dried fruit.

Variation: Amaretto-spiked Mincemeat

If you like a really booze-flavored mixture, then add 1 to 2 tablespoons amaretto liqueur in addition to the brandy.

MINI-MINCEMEAT PALMIERS

These palmiers are a slightly more lady-like offering than traditional mince pies; they look beautiful dusted with confectioners' (icing) sugar and would be great to serve after dinner with coffee. They are easy to make and also freeze well—just reheat them in a hot oven and serve immediately.

Makes about 24
9oz (225g) Boozy Mincemeat (see page 165)
1 roll from a 15oz (425g) pack of frozen ready-rolled puff pastry, defrosted
all-purpose flour, for rolling
confectioners' (icing) sugar, for dusting
ground cinnamon, for dusting (optional)

Put the mincemeat into a food processor and pulse on and off until it forms a spreadable paste.

Unroll the pastry on its baking sheet, then dust with a little flour. Roll out to form a square. Spread the mincemeat evenly all over the pastry, right up to the edges, then, using the baking sheet to help you, roll up from two opposite sides so that you have two long sausage shapes side by side. Gently squeeze the two edges together so that they keep their shape but don't unroll. Wrap loosely with the baking sheet, transfer to a plate and chill for 30 minutes. Meanwhile, preheat the oven to 400°F (200°C).

Remove the palmier roll from the fridge, unwrap, and, using a small sharp knife, carefully cut the roll into ½in (1cm) slices. Place onto a non-stick baking sheet and bake for 15 minutes, or until golden and cooked.

Transfer immediately to a wire rack to cool slightly. Dust with confectioners' (icing) sugar (or a mix of confectioners' sugar and cinnamon) and serve, warm, on a plate.

If you want to freeze the palmiers, cool completely and place in a lidded plastic container between layers of parchment paper. When you are ready, put the frozen palmiers onto a baking sheet and reheat them for a few minutes in a hot oven.

Conversion Chart

Weight (solids)

7g = ¼oz	
10g = ½oz	
20g = ¾oz	
25g = 1oz	
40g = 1½oz	
50g = 2oz	
60g = 2 ½oz	
75g = 3oz	
100g = 3½oz	
110g = 4oz (¼lb)	
125g = 4½oz	
150g = 5½oz	
175g = 6oz	
200g = 7oz	
225g = 8oz (½lb)	
250g = 9oz	
275g = 10oz	
300g = 10½oz	
310g = 11oz	
325g = 11½oz	
350g = 12oz (¾lb)	
375g = 13oz	
400g = 14oz	

425g = 15oz
450g = 1lb
500g (½kg) = 18oz
600g = 1¼lb
700g = 1½lb
750g = 1lb 10oz
900g = 2lb
1kg = 2¼lb
1.1kg = 2½lb
1.2kg = 2lb 12oz
1.3kg = 3lb
1.5kg = 3lb 5oz
1.6kg = 3½lb
1.8kg = 4lb
2kg = 4lb 8oz
2.25kg = 5lb
2.5kg = 5lb 8oz
3kg = 6lb 8oz

Volume (liquids)

5ml = 1 teaspoon
10ml = 2 teaspoons
15ml = 1 tablespoon
   or ½fl oz

30ml = 1fl oz
40ml = 1½fl oz
50ml = 2fl oz
60ml = 2½fl oz
75ml = 3fl oz
100ml = 3½fl oz
125ml = 4fl oz
150ml = 5fl oz
160ml = 5½fl oz
175ml = 6fl oz
200ml = 7fl oz
225ml = 8fl oz
250ml (0.25 liter) = 9fl oz
300ml = 10fl oz
325ml = 11fl oz
350ml = 12fl oz
370ml = 13fl oz
400ml = 14fl oz
425ml = 15fl oz
450ml = 16fl oz
500ml (½ quart) = 18fl oz
550ml = 19fl oz
600ml = 20fl oz
700ml = ¾ quart

1 liter = 1 quart
1.5 liters = 1½ quarts
2 liters = 2 quarts

Length

5mm = ¼in
1cm = ½in
2cm = ¾in
2.5cm = 1in
3cm = 1¼in
4cm = 1½in
5cm = 2in
7.5 cm = 3in
10cm = 4in
15cm = 6in
18cm = 7in
20cm = 8in
24cm = 10in
28cm = 11in
30cm = 12in

Oven Temperatures

Celsius	Farenheit	Description
110°C	225°F	cool
120°C	250°F	cool
130°C	275°F	very low
150°C	300°F	very low
160°C	325°F	low
180°C	350°F	moderate
190°C	375°F	mod. hot
200°C	400°F	hot
220°C	425°F	hot
230°C	450°F	very hot
240°C	475°F	very hot

Resources

Canada

Canadian Tire
www.canadiantire.ca
• Mason jars, jelly bags, strawberry huller, canning wax, fruit jar rings, canning labels, peelers, juicers, strainers, jar lifters, other canning equipment.
• Available in-store throughout Canada.

USA

Target
www.target.com
• mason jars, crystal jelly jars, manner jar racks, peelers, canner kits, pressure cookers/canners, canning and pickling salt, canning labels, juicers, strainers, jar lifters, other canning equipment.
• Available in-store and online throughout US.

Kitchen Krafts
The Foodcrafter's Supply Catalog
PO Box 442
Waukon, IA 52172-0442
PHONE: 1-800-298-5389 or 1-563-535-8000
EMAIL: service@kitchenkrafts.com
http://www.kitchenkrafts.com

• Water bath canners, pressure canners, juicers, peelers, fruit pectin, ClearJel starch, Ball canning jars, canning labels, apple peelers, cider presses, food strainers, canning equipment, cherry pitters etc.
• Deliver throughout US and around the world.

Canning Pantry
Highland Brands, LLC
19 N. 100 W.
Hyrum, UT 84319
PHONE: 435-245-6776
www.canningpantry.com

• Canning/pickling equipment and supplies.
• Only ships within US and Canada.

Canning Supply
A division of Kitchen Krafts, Inc.
1478 Elon Drive
Waterville, IA 52170
PHONE: 1-888-612-1950 or 1-563-535-8004
www.canningsupply.com

• Home canning equipment and supplies.
• Only ships within US.

Australia

Redback Trading Company
PO Box 1101
Kensington, Victoria
Australia, 3031
PHONE: (03) 9378 2963
EMAIL: info@redbacktrading.com.au
www.redbacktrading.com.au

• Strainers, strainer bags, jars, lids, pectin, etc.
• Only ships within Australia.

UK

Lakeland
Alexandra Buildings
Windermere
Cumbria LA23 1BQ
TEL: 01539 488 100
www.lakeland.co.uk

• Labels, jars, lids, thermometers, waxed circles, strainers, funnels, cookbooks, Kilner discs.
• Over 40 stores throughout the UK. They do deliver overseas (for an additional cost), although there are restrictions on some items.

Acknowledgments

Creature Comforts

EMAIL: creaturecomfortsblog@gmail.com

http://www.creaturecomfortsblog.com

This design-led blog gives tips and tricks for making your own crafts of all varieties, as well as beautiful projects and free download materials. Their downloadable labels would look great on your homemade jam pots, making them ideal as gifts.

Jam Jar Shop

Unit 2, 24 Pillings Road
Oakham
Rutland LE15 6QF
TEL: 01572 720720
EMAIL: sales@jamjarshop.com
www.jamjarshop.com

• Jam jars, labels, equipment, ingredients, packaging, etc.
• UK delivery only.

Cakes, Cookies & Crafts Shop

Morris Holbon Ltd,
Unit 5, Woodgate Park,
White Lund Industrial Estate,
Morecambe,
Lancashire.
LA3 3PS
TEL: 01524 389684
www.cakescookiesandcraftsshop.co.uk

• Jam thermometers, stainless steel funnels, and straining bags, jars, labels, etc.
• Deliver overseas.

Enormous thanks to:

All those family and friends who donated their precious family recipes, tested boiling pots of jam in the middle of summer, and offered advice and reasurrance—Jenny the limoncello connoisseur, Emily Bray, Al Studd, Simon and Vanessa Baker, Penny Williams, Clare Evelyn, Melissa Clegg, Judy Snell, Isobel Sanderson, Lesley Sanderson, Delia Montgomery, Andrea Elles, Valerie Barratt, Sue Coltart, Guy Cox, Miranda Chetwode, Claire Davies, Aly Godman, Sophie Hill, Sophie Denby, Auntie Gay, Sarah Prior, Anna del Conte, Alex Mackay, Reverend Kevin Mentzel, and especially my mom, brother, Hilary James, Jen Reynolds, and Tania MacCullam, who really went beyond the call of duty.

Claire Davies, for ultra scrupulous proof reading.

Henhurst farm shop for their wonderful produce, Lakeland for their endless supply of jam jars and jelly bags and Emily Bray for letting me raid her veggie patch!

Karen Pilkington for being so highly organized, allowing us to shoot at your house, and for being such a fantastic new food stylist!

My mother and Iain for allowing us to shoot the book at Bishopsdale Oast. The bed and breakfast with its stunning garden and veggie patch made our lives very easy when it came to finding beautiful subject matter!

To Kyle for offering me the book in the first place, Jenny, my book editor and Catharine, her assistant.

And finally to the most fantastic photographer Laura Hynd, an awesome stylist Cynthia Inions, and book designer Jim Smith whose combined talents really have made the book.

Index